Deirdre Macken is a journalist, columnist and author. She has written for the *Australian Financial Review*, *The Sydney Morning Herald* and its colour magazine *Good Weekend*, *The Age*, and, currently, *The Australian*.

Praise for
Growing Grapes Might Be Fun

'Deirdre Macken's memoir is more than a lively account of turning unpromising, trash-strewn hectares into a productive vineyard. It's a reflection on family, community and the rewards of caring for the land that sustains us.'

Geraldine Brooks, Pulitzer Prize winning author

'I simply adored reading this account of a life-change with a purpose, laden with honesty and Deirdre's characteristic wit. Above all, I won't forget the love on display or city–rural wisdom gained. All that's left is to try the wine!'

Geraldine Doogue, ABC presenter

growing grapes might be fun

Deirdre Macken

ALLEN&UNWIN

SYDNEY · MELBOURNE · AUCKLAND · LONDON

First published in 2023

Allen & Unwin
Cammeraygal Country
83 Alexander Street
Crows Nest NSW 2065
Australia
Phone: (61 2) 8425 0100
Email: info@allenandunwin.com
Web: www.allenandunwin.com

*Allen & Unwin acknowledges the Traditional Owners of the Country on which we
live and work. We pay our respects to all Aboriginal and Torres Strait Islander
Elders, past and present.*

A catalogue record for this
book is available from the
National Library of Australia

ISBN 978 1 76106 770 9

Set in 12.25/19.75 pt Goudy Old Style by Bookhouse, Sydney
Printed and bound in Australia by the Opus Group

10 9 8 7 6 5 4 3 2 1

The paper in this book is FSC® certified.
FSC® promotes environmentally responsible,
socially beneficial and economically viable
management of the world's forests.

This book is dedicated to my husband,
Roger Johnstone

Contents

1 Dumpsville   1

2 Starting with a Scratch   10

3 Cross-stitching the Country   17

4 Breathe In, Breathe Out, Unpack   24

5 Old Enough to Know Better   31

6 Pumped for Planting   37

7 Stick by Stick   43

8 Hard Graft   52

9 Winded   58

10 Back to School for a Continent   66

11 An Imaginary Friend   73

12 The Dry   81

13 Husband Gets a Fridge Magnet   89

14 Pitter Patter   95

15 You Don't Know Me, but You Know My Mum   99

16 Locals Only   109

17 A Bake-off   117

18 Boring My Kid, Blooding the Next Gen   124

19 Recollections of Rubbish   131

20 Show and Tell Too Much   138

21 Succession: Too Soon and Not Soon Enough   147

22 A Feast for the Apocalypse   154

23 Do My Underpants Look Big Here?   162

24 Betsy, Zoe and Parsley Arrive   168

25 Dumpsville Revisited   175

26 Dinner on the Hoof   182

27 The Pantone Farmer   189

28 A Silent Shame   197

29 My BOM is Better than Yours   204

30 The Boys are Back in Town   209

31 The Ghost Within   217

32 Plein Air   223

33 Netscape   231

34 A Ragtag of Design   236

35 Letting Go   241

36 Harvest à Go-go   246

37 Illegal Still   253

38 Fermenting   260

39 A Name to Forget   265

40 Wine Prose   271

41 The Call of Country   277

Epilogue   287

Acknowledgements   293

1

Dumpsville

The place is a dump. And it has been for decades, judging by the layers of debris that spread out hundreds of metres all around the house. Piles of the forgotten, the failed and the maybe-one-day are spread wide and deep—at least half a metre deep. If you started digging anywhere here, you would discover the archaeology of defeat. And possibly a body or two.

The junk is visible on Google Earth's satellite image of the property like a dark ink splash dropped from space, as my husband Roger and I discovered a few days previously when we tried to place the property on a map of New South Wales. You can see the two clapped-out tractors, an industrial freezer, four derelict cars, a half-constructed yacht hanging off the side of the woolshed, a shipping container, a wonky wool spreader, skeletons of industrial equipment and a horse-drawn buggy with metal-rimmed wheels laid to rest near a wood pile. You can imagine the Google Earth god shaking a finger at the litterers: go clean up your room!

But on the ground, it's the scraps of junk that catch the eye. Twine, broken glass, a battered basin, plastic containers full of toxic concoctions, webbing, plastic sheeting, broken bikes, pots, cutlery, pipes, hoses, car accessories, wheelbarrows from almost every decade of the twentieth century, conduit, toys, picnic furniture, fencing, nails, bottles and cans strewn across the land and embedded in the soil.

'There's a lot of junk still here.' I shouldn't have said it but the relaxed look on the face of the previous owner, Henri, roiled me.

'A lot of it has gone,' he says, pointing to brown patches where automobiles had lain for decades.

'It would be good if you can shift a few more things, Henri.' My mother, Ann, is always the diplomat but perhaps she also knows that confrontation isn't going to convince Henri to clean up a century of neglect.

It is our first inspection of Cockatoo Hill in December 2016 and for my mother, Roger and me it isn't a pleasant experience. This is no Insta-moment. This is not a love-at-first-sight moment that would send city folk into the nearest country outfitters store to declare: 'Give me the whole R.M. Williams kit, I'm heading bush.' It looks more like a Tip Change than a Tree Change.

My mother and her husband Ray have owned Cockatoo Hill, a 100-hectare property outside of Yass, for a year. It is named for its most prominent feature and is curious-looking because its conical shape is almost denuded of vegetation. A mean observer might say it looks like a giant pimple but it does have a creek flowing around its base, and on a plateau halfway down the Hill sits a house—a house that hasn't been loved in a long time. For a year, Mum has allowed the previous owner access, partly to ease his transition out of a long-held family property, partly to encourage him to clean it up and partly because she wasn't sure what she was going to do with the place. Ann already runs several grazing properties in the area and Cockatoo Hill has been home to flocks of sheep for as long as local memory records. But Ann has other ideas—for the Hill and for us.

Most of Cockatoo Hill would remain a grazing property, but Roger, who has recently retired, could help her establish a vineyard on a few hectares of the property. After all, she explained a few weeks ago, a local vigneron had commented that the soils looked good for growing wine grapes and Roger liked to drink wine. Surely that was good enough reason for a vineyard.

Can a farming enterprise start like that? Just two suppositions and a can-do attitude? Would you call that a business plan? I'm not sure, but I'm prepared to muddle around with the idea if only because it's something new. And it's something to do. Roger is at a loss after taking redundancy from his lifetime career and Mum hates seeing resources—including human ones—go to waste. Besides Roger, as a former newspaper and magazine editor, has natural project management skills and Mum loves a new project, especially one that might introduce her to a new industry and an interesting community like the one involved in wine-making. She may want to see more of her daughter too.

While the previous owner picks up a few odds and ends that he forgot to pick up half a century ago, Mum and Roger survey the land. They look at aspect, contours, water channels, rocky areas (there are lots of those) and tree canopies. They are imagining a future vineyard; redrawing this land with their imagination and a few plastic bags of soil samples. I try to follow their exploration, picturing myself in a floral dress with a wicker basket full of freshly picked roses and figs, ready to greet guests to the vineyard.

But I can only see the ink splash of junk. As they chat about aspects of the land, my eyes keep being snagged by rubbish. I can't see the landscape for the litter and I can't not see the litter. Everywhere I look there is stuff that needs to be cleared, and I'm beginning to fume over the circumstances that created it. This land isn't mine but I'm offended at what has been done to it.

Sheep stare at the visitors wandering around their hill, perhaps wondering how much of their space is going to be invaded, and it occurs to me that they and their ancestors have resided here far longer than the span of my life. This has been sheep country since shortly after 1824, when Hamilton Hume found a way to get from Sydney to Melbourne with the hapless Hovell in his wake. What made it sheep country? A market for wool in England. A need for meat in the new colony. A lack of any other ideas?

Wool is the default enterprise for this area, but newcomers are finding different purposes for this stretch of Australia. A few kilometres away grows an olive grove that looks to be a few decades old. It was probably planted in the 1980s when Australians discovered the Mediterranean diet. In the next town, some people are putting in organic barley to be used in the craft beer boom. Last year, a friend, who has a property 100 kilometres to the north of here, talked of planting oak trees on her land so truffles could be grown around their roots. As I watch the sheep retreat further up the Hill, I notice the boulders of lichen-spotted granite scattered across the hillside. One day, this Hill might be a rock farm.

People have been finding different uses for land since they got sick of hunting and gathering. Land is the last frontier, a free expression of enterprise, unhampered by planning policies, neighbourhood sensitivities or any proof you can actually do it. We can do what we bloody well like, whether the sheep like it or not.

But first the land has to be restored to its natural state and I develop a plan—a makeover plan. I will be the garbo— something my mother threatened us with when we failed to study hard enough at school. For however long it takes, I will leave my floral dresses in Sydney and don those work pants with pockets everywhere and hooks for hanging stuff off.

I have a strategy. I will start on the edges of the ink splash and move towards the centre. The centre being a battered asbestos house that began the twentieth century as a modest cottage but had extrusions added at various points, perhaps when the residents had more faith in improving their lot.

The house will be last on the agenda because it may need a wrecking ball. Although it looks like a single house from the driveway, it has obviously been used as a duplex since an extension was added in the 1970s. The oldest half of the house resembles a dosshouse because it looks like a place where those who've been beaten by life throw their bodies down to rest at night without much confidence that they will rise again in the morning. The 'modern' extension that has been joined onto the southern side of the old cottage—a bathroom, tiny kitchen, two bedrooms and a lounge—is more habitable but charm is not a feature.

Starting at the edges has a few advantages. The junk is less thick, so I can get a quicker satisfaction hit. I can look back at a tiny parcel of land and think: *Today that is better, that little bit of land has been returned to the landscape.* As Roger and Mum settle their discussions on an eastern hill, I map out the terrain for clearing and imagine a weight lifting off the landscape. It will be like removing a net from the neck of a dolphin. The land will breathe again. It will regain its dignity when it's allowed it to be land again—just land, lying under the sun, doing its work with photosynthesis, buzzing with insects, pecked at by birds, trodden on by sheep, sucking up rain, turning hard with frost and staring at the night sky. I breathe easier too.

One day I am going to look out over that land and see the contour of hills, read the history of the giant gums in their misshapen limbs, scour the sky for the birds making strange songs, watch the sheep grazing across weed-free pastures, notice the rivulets made by summer rain and not see any junk. One day I may even see a vineyard in the landscape.

❧

As Henri mooches around, I try not to be judgemental. It's too easy to make judgements on people for the stuff they leave behind. It's enough to surmise that, at some stage, this property defeated its owners—from the accretion of junk, I'm guessing that time was in the 1970s or '80s. Maybe they got sick. Maybe they started fighting with each other and lost the will to create a happy place. There could have been problems over the ownership. Whatever happened, junk has a pernicious habit. Once a bit of it is lying around, it attracts more. Once more is added, the pile becomes the place where stuff is left. Soon it's too much to clear away and, eventually, you no longer see it.

I can't *unsee* it.

I've often wondered why some rural properties end up looking like dumps while others look like the background for an R.M. Williams catalogue. Driving past properties that are littered with broken tractors, buggies, discarded cars and cages that may have once held chickens or dogs—or, gulp, children—I speculate on how they ended up that way. Poverty is one explanation. Depression another. Maybe the owner became disabled or was abandoned by family. They could be hoarders or tinkerers, or maybe they just woke up one day and couldn't see what was happening to their place any longer. In the city, problems like these are mostly hidden; in the country some mental health problems can be spotted from the roadside.

We gather around the cars on our exit and Henri says, 'So I'm making a sea change (pointing to the yacht), and you're making a tree change.'

No, we're obviously making a tip change and, if you don't shift your half-made yacht off this property soon, your sea change is going down to the local tip.

That's what I had wanted to say, but I didn't. I'm learning. In the country you don't look to make enemies. The community is small and memories long and, hey, it doesn't get the job done.

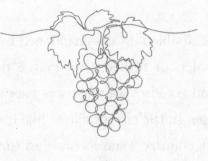

2

Starting with a Scratch

I can't recall how the idea of farming arose. I was no fan of the wide brown land. And it is usually brown. When I thought of farming, I thought of people who'd had the misfortune of being born outside of the city and had been forced to toughen up to survive to adulthood in the back of beyond (which began inland of the last espresso machine). Sure, those people were admirable for the fact that they had stayed out there throughout the Dorothea Mackellar horrors and continued to deliver the skim milk for my latte and the greenery for my poke bowl, but farmers were as mysterious to me as people from some cultural communities in the city—I didn't get why they did some things.

When Mum took up farming in the 1990s, I was mysti-
fied and a little worried that there might be a farmer gene
in our family that could manifest at any time and convince
me to flee the city. She was, after all, a professor at a major
university and she'd fought many battles to get that mortar-
board on her head. When she had started back at university
in the early 1970s, she still had ten children living at home
and was a newly divorced woman. For the next fifteen-odd
years, she was an academic, a property investor, a mother
and the wife of a doctor, who had six children of his own.
Then she decided to become a farmer.

She was sixty-five years old—well almost, and acutely
aware that, after her sixty-fifth birthday, the university would
pressure her to retire, and she might be expected to knit.
Or play bowls. Mum was never going to play bowls. She
didn't play at anything. She worked, she never wanted to
stop working and she couldn't understand why others wanted
to stop working.

She juggled her full-time university job with farming for
the first few years and managed to quell suggestions of a
retirement whenever colleagues or university bureaucrats
suggested it. On one of her visits to her first grandchildren
(mine!), I remember telling her that she'd get a better return
on her money from a savings account. Save yourself the toil,
risk, hardship, weed control, snake danger, fire threat, ruined

complexion and the grinding despair of drought—just put your money in the bank and take a cruise. I was blunt about it, but only because I wanted to save her from the horrors we had seen featured in headlines about country life.

Mum replied that she liked being creative with her money; she liked the fact that she was growing food for people and she liked the fact that the capital value of the land was always increasing. She was right. Then and even more later.

When I was in a more diplomatic mood, I would admit that 'winegrowing might be fun'. As I said this, I'd imagine lounging under a sandstone loggia roof, overlooking folds of hills striped with vines. I'd be clothed in linen and surrounded by friends with tumblers of the wine that we'd picked in last year's harvest, discussing its characteristics, the influence of terroir and whether to open another bottle. Cypress trees would stand sentinel on the horizon. Roosters would crow in the distance, mist would lift off the hills like a silk dress dancing and stray notes from a classical concert would drift on the breeze. That's the sort of farming I like.

When I tore my mind away from the Tuscan hillside, I'd admit that winegrowing in Australia was an exercise in losing money graciously. Retired executives might do it for the tax deduction, scientists might do it for a hobby, big companies did it with lots of machinery, but little wine growers did it because they're foolish. It's like a big country garden—the returns aren't fiscal, even if they can be fun.

The fantasy of vineyard life played around at the back of my mind on trips to Europe and the US, on car trips through wine regions of Australia and around the dinner table with friends. It was great as a fantasy, certainly better than taking up a hobby like drawing, painting or singing in a community choir (all of which I am hopeless at). Then came redundancy. Mine and my husband's. It was an earlier retirement than we'd envisioned. A reluctant retirement, even if the redundancy was requested. You could call it unemployment, except that we had enough savings to live on and we were too old to catch attention on a Seek listing.

It took a year of kicking the tyres of retirement before we found ourselves inspecting a hillside of junk, mentally pegging out a vineyard. In between our sudden exit from full-time work and our appearance on the Hill, there was a business that Roger started, worked on, launched and gently folded with the illness of his partner. I got some gigs, snagged a regular column in *The Australian* and dipped into business writing, literary judging and family history writing.

It sounds a lot, but it wasn't enough. Our Sydney home got buffed, our golf handicaps came down, the wheel rims of my car got polished. But it wasn't enough. We both felt lost. Is there anything worse than having energy but no outlet? Having ideas but no application; having something to contribute and nothing to contribute to; looking in from the outside when you once were an insider?

My mother, bless her, couldn't abide it. We were her greatest nightmare—productive people without a purpose. She also loved us. So, she thought, we might not like to run sheep or cattle on the wide brown land; we'd said we'd consider a vineyard. She had the land; we had the energy and we knew how to navigate YouTube. The Hill was on the edge of Canberra's winegrowing area, and one of the area's greatest winemakers had mentioned in passing that the land might be good for grapes.

Besides, we'd talked a lot about wine over the years. Terroir, aspect, grape varieties—those were some of the terms Roger and I tossed around over dinner with friends. We'd visited enough regional wineries over the years. Australian and overseas. We'd even helped friends pick grapes early in our retirement period. Were we wine wankers? Probably.

As the idea of a vineyard mulled, we began searching online for tips on how to grow grapes and what to look for in a vineyard. An east or north-east facing aspect. A gentle slope but not too steep. Not too close to depressions where frosts settle; land clear of rocks—mostly—and free of trees or shade. Access to water—either bore, dam or creek. Soil with a pH of 6 to 8.

Why? What makes a professor-farmer and two under-employed journalists think they can grow grapes—grapes that will become wine that people will want to drink? I don't imagine picking up a scalpel and doing surgery. I don't imagine getting a pile of receipts and preparing a tax return for a client. I can't design a bridge, dig a mine, teach a class of five-year-olds, deliver a woman's baby or build a house. At that time, I couldn't change a tap washer and, if my computer weirded out, the only solution I could come up with was to turn it off and on.

And yet winegrowing has been an amateur game since the Romans took their god Bacchus with them throughout Europe. Wine was a daily libation for the gentry in the Middle Ages; vines were a feature of every backyard in Italy for centuries and were grown by German immigrants in Australia's early days, especially in South Australia. Winegrowing had become a hobby for CSIRO scientists around Canberra in the 1970s and a little later by rich businessmen dabbling at it in the hills outside Sydney and Melbourne.

The latest pioneers are the hipsters moving out of inner cities to hills in Tasmania, Victoria and New South Wales to become makers in the agricultural space. They grow or, more often, source grapes to make natural wines—just the way wine was made in European villages throughout the centuries. This wave of winemakers is redefining the industry, splitting off the business of grape growing from the business of winemaking, splitting winemaking from tradition. They range over the country, buying grapes from growers and borrowing space from wineries to make and store their wines, and then marketing their wines through online sites or fetes. Or by begging a spot on a shelf from independent wine shops or by turning up at restaurants with a few bottles and a story to tell.

Through the centuries many people have thought about giving wine growing a go. Roger and I might have been more clueless, we were certainly older, but we belonged to a tradition. And the weird thing is that grape vines are easy to grow—in fact, some think they're harder to kill than grow—but it's really hard to grow grapes that will become wine that people will want to drink. And that's something that we won't know for another four or five years.

I guess that's the most important part of the wine-growing experience. It's not capital, nor expertise, it's not even networks or an encouraging mum. It's hope. A big well of hope.

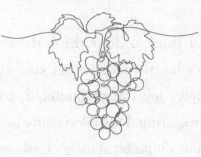

3

Cross-stitching the Country

My sister Mary and I are removing rubbish, and for the past hour we've been labouring over a rusty water tank. Although it's partly flattened, it's too big to put onto the ute's tray for the next run to the Waste Transfer Station, otherwise known as The Tip. So, we have to reduce its size. Somehow.

We decided to cut it up and the only tool we could think of using was pliers. We've been crouching on the ground cutting this giant tank with small pliers for an hour. As I wrestle with the cutting action and bending the cut parts back to continue to work my way across the tank, I have had time to think.

Here's what I think: I don't think these are the right tools for the job, but then I have no idea what a job like this requires. Every job I've encountered at the farm is a new challenge, requiring skills I don't have and tools I don't know about. *How do people do this?* I ask myself. Then I think, *Well, they obviously do things like this or the country- side would be full of rusty old tanks.*

Next thought: *What tool should be used to reduce the size of a 22,000-litre tank? Scissors, pliers, chainsaw, hammer, crowbar? Or is there something you can buy at the rural supplies store in town?* I ponder how foolish I would feel going into the rural supplies store and asking for a tank-cutting tool. It would give them a laugh, and I don't need to give blokes another reason to laugh at women.

My choice of tool derives from being an urban, middle- aged female professional who has few practical skills beyond the Tools tab on her computer. I also have a fridge covered with magnets from tradies who can fix a leaky tap, mend a length of deck timber, install a device, clean windows, fix grouting or clear a gutter. That's what city people do: they call for help. So, when faced with having to fix something, or reduce the size of a tank so it can fit on the back of a ute, my only solution is to get a scissors-type thing and cut it up.

Thus, my sister and I are crouched over this rusty tank, looking like we're cutting out the pattern for an automobile.

I had hoped that Mary would have a better solution, if only because she has been living in the country for a few years now. It turns out she's hardly more equipped than me because she has spent her career as a linguist and only has a few books and many academic papers, conferences and PhD students to her bow. If we could talk this tank onto the back of a ute, we'd be the perfect people for the job.

The other thing that occurs to me, as I try to avoid being cut by the galvanised iron, is to ask whether this tank really is a water tank. I stand up to stretch and look at the tank carefully. It's very brown, but that's rust, right? They didn't use galvanised iron tanks for septics, did they? Surely, they'd rust. Or cave in. Or something. I realise I have no idea what a septic tank is made of.

I glance down the Hill to where Roger and the fencer Ian are building the infrastructure for the vineyard. They have tools—tools that can dig, tools that determine a straight line to a distant post, tools that can tighten wire. They look as if they know what they're doing. Not for the first time, I wonder how blokes get the clean jobs and I end up wrestling with stuff that's messy and possibly toxic. I suggest a coffee break to Mary and she agrees.

As we wander inside, avoiding the hazards of old pipes, wires, broken furniture and pots that still litter the surrounds of the house, I feel immensely grateful that Mary is willing to be my garbo apprentice. It's a lonely job, and so far I have filled three giant skips, done about thirty ute trips to the tip and held a couple of burn-offs. Yet I've still not reached the inner circle of junk in the house compound. I've also busted fingernails, practised my stock of curses and coarsened the skin on my hands to a crocodile texture as I've inched slowly from the outskirts of neglect towards the house—a house I hope might be demolished or carried away in a southerly storm. During that time, when friends have asked me what I'm contributing to the tree change, I've replied, 'Garbology.' And I'm not ashamed of it.

Which is strange really. Because I've been a senior journalist, working among business leaders and politicians, academics and professionals, using big words and wearing smart clothes and bringing in a salary that afforded a nice home, enabled the raising of three children and even paid for the odd holiday to those nightmare theme parks up the coast. I had business cards. But suddenly I have a borrowed ute and Bunnings gloves—big meaty gloves—and lots of them, because I keep losing them in the back of the ute. And, yet, I found the work strangely satisfying. Maybe I'd missed my calling as a garbo.

Half an hour later, when Mary and I return to the job, the tank has disappeared. I look at the ute tray and there it is—folded like an origami box on the back. Roger comes up when he sees us staring at the neat package.

'Ian did it,' he says. 'You should have seen it. He just bought his tractor up, used its bucket to bend the metal into smaller and smaller parts, and plonked it on the back of the ute. It was amazing to watch.'

Ian is amazing to watch, especially when he's in his tractor. Over the months ahead, we will get to see Ian and his tractor plough up fields, carry loads of poles and wire, shift heavy junk around the property, take down a huge tree that had been split in two in a storm and gently move a hive of bees from a dead tree that needed to be removed. He uses the tractor—an eight-tonne, craggy-looking machine—like an extra hand. It's an extension of his body in a way that suggests either confidence or a lifetime of use. Or both. The morning I watched him take down the giant split tree was like watching a ballet performance. He'd manoeuvre the machine into place then raise the forks and pull, twist or nudge the branches to the ground. Then another deft twist of the machine and the next branch would be coaxed to the ground.

If I'm sounding impressed, it may be because Roger and I were trying to learn how to operate a much smaller tractor with two sets of gears. Or maybe there were two engines. Whatevs. It had lots of safety devices, attachments that seemed impossible to grapple with, instruments that got cranky whenever you didn't pay attention and levers that might have been for operating the giant bucket or turning on the air conditioning. If Ian operates his tractor like a surgeon with an eight-tonne scalpel, we operate ours like a Rubik's cube while being colour blind.

But Roger and I shouldn't have been surprised. Our brains had been formed by decades of using them for reading, writing, arguing, extrapolating and representing. The neural pathways to words and images were so well travelled they were like highways, while the pathways to the physical world of machines, shape shifting, building and connecting things were so atrophied you'd be pushed to describe them as goat tracks. Our neural pathways for solving practical problems only led to the magnets on the fridge.

City skills, country skills. You sort of know they're different, but it's only away from the latte belt that I realise what a great gulf there is between the two and how useless some skills are when you take them elsewhere. In the country, my city skills are peripheral—nice to have during a coffee break, but not necessary for the jobs of a farm. And sometimes they just serve to alert country folk to the presence of an outsider. Ian's country skills wouldn't transfer easily to the city, but only because they are too broad to fit on a fridge magnet. Ian is a fencer, machine operator, excavator, surveyor, grader, tree lopper, sheep and pig farmer, shearer, orchardist, plumber, mechanic, rubbish removalist, fencer. And he might even manage a tractor ballet routine if asked nicely.

Ian doesn't just shape his environment, he is shaped by it. Heavy-set, with a hesitant smile and muscular hands, he is something of a tracker. He will point out that the farm gate has been hitched to the third notch and therefore a certain person has probably made a visit (he knows we set it to the loosest notch and I don't think he approves). He will note tyre tracks on our muddy driveway and ask if we've had a big delivery recently. He knows the local gossip, if only because he is related to so many locals. He also mentally tracks the animals, birds, watercourses and bits of junk that might be useful for fixing stuff. He's too big for a fridge magnet, but we've got his number and we know we can call him every time we have a problem. We're already good friends with Ian.

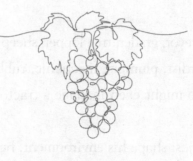

4

Breathe In, Breathe Out, Unpack

We commute from Sydney every week or two. Leaving Sydney at dawn as the morning peak traffic builds, we scamper just ahead of the snarls and jockeying that mark the start of the day for five million people. It takes an hour to drive from our home to the southern reaches of the city, and it's only when we leave the tract housing behind that we realise how tight our shoulders have been held, how vigilant we have been. It can feel as if we are being sling-shotted out of the city into clear air. By the time we pass through the highlands of the south and enter farming land, it's like we've exhaled the city and begun inhaling the land. I wonder if it's possible to expand at a cellular level.

Three hours later, we step out of the car onto 100 hec-tares. For a city person, that's a lot of space. That amount of land in the city would house a suburb of 10,000 people in large houses. It's big enough to need binoculars to view the boundary and expansive enough to defeat a jog across it, especially as most of it is hilly. Just one hill really. A crumb if you're looking from space, a mountain if you're looking up from the house. The Hill has a trig station at the top that measures its height and does whatever trigs are meant to do, and the topography fans out at its base, allowing both trees and sheep to get a foothold.

The Hill's shape is noticeable because it has little vegetation at its peak. It looks like it's been through chemotherapy, dotted with tufts of dead trees and the odd grove of living trees that have survived storms, sheep grazing and lightning strikes. It has rocks too: boulders leaning precariously out from the folds of land or lumped together unconvincingly. Someone suggested it might be an ancient volcano, possibly because of its shape or maybe because the rocks look like they've been blasted from their natural sequence. It hasn't had tree cover in many years, possibly centuries.

Locals have stories about this Hill. Some say it's where the Ngunnawal people held look-out for settlers approaching, and certainly you can see for many kilometres from its peak. Today you can look down on farms, creeks, a highway and

25

remnant bush where in years past you would have spotted campfires, cattle drives, buggies and a posse of settlers, who might have had bad intentions. Others have suggested that the first explorers, Hume and Hovell, used this Hill to survey the valley for fertile farming land and a route to Melbourne. And, if you know in which direction to look, you can see the roof of the cottage where Hamilton Hume settled after he made the tracks for the Hume Highway. It has history, this Hill, but it feels older than history. It feels like it needs to be respected, and sometimes it feels like it needs to be mourned.

Mostly, when we step out of the car and unpack, it just feels like an arrival. Not that we've arrived home but that we have come to a place where we breathe more easily, more slowly; a place where we feel ourselves expanding into the landscape. This is a place where the eye can graze the horizon and the lungs feel caressed by the air. We listen too; we listen to the sounds of distant tractors, of nearby birds and of wind in old gums. Sometimes frogs, but not too often—the weather has been mostly dry recently, some say ominously dry.

For a city person, it takes a while to feel confident in such an expanse of nature and the first few visits can be scary. Too big, too quiet, too empty of easy reference points. You tread carefully—snakes! You listen for passing cars and wonder if they are friend or foe, or just a passing car. The foreign landscape is a setting for scary stories.

At night we listen to strange noises. Wind belting up the Hill and teasing tall trees. Animals scampering around the edges of the house or on top of the iron roof. The creak of old boards, suggesting footfalls or a monster hidden under the boards. I have a nightmare in which an earth tremor loosens a giant boulder up the Hill. I listen to it crunching over trees and roaring down the Hill towards the house. In the morning I look up the Hill to make sure it was a nightmare.

When we tidy up outside, we pull weeds that inevitably sting or prick. We lift materials that hide colonies of spiders, mostly redbacks. We dig holes for plants, hoping the earth isn't disguising electric cables. Even the machinery on the farm seems to have many ways of killing you. Especially those air-conditioning levers on the tractor.

❧

One day, still cleaning up junk, my sister Mary and I wandered to the edge of the paddock to inspect two couches that had been dumped by a previous owner. Who travels a couple of hundred metres into a paddock to dump couches? We noticed the ground near the dumped couches had been trenched deeply and, quite accurately, I observed 'I think that's where dead sheep are buried.'

'But what else is buried there?' asked Mary.

'It would be easy to bury bodies here,' I unwisely replied.

'There's room for lots of bodies,' Mary said.

Mary was reverting to childhood, when she was always the one to terrify her younger sisters and brothers. 'Bloody bones in the woodshed!' she would proclaim. It doesn't sound scary now and I'm not sure why it was scary then. Now that I think of it, I don't even know what it referred to. But it became the bogeyman of our youth and when Mary said it we would run screaming for Mum.

Mary and I were still teasing each other with talk of bodies and serial killers when we turned around to walk back and discovered an old ute had just parked up the Hill. A big man in a black hat was getting out of the car and staring towards us. Just staring. Waiting.

'Do you know him?' I whispered.

'No. You?'

'No.'

As he began to move towards us, I noted that his car was blocking the only exit from the property. Like a detective, I scanned for threats—the black hat, the man looming up the Hill, the ute parked askew across the exit, the door of the ute ajar, so he could reach in and grab . . . something.

The only missing element was the soundtrack to spaghetti westerns—drums, whistling birds and howling coyotes. We slowed our pace as he began walking towards us, both of us thinking: Escape routes! Weapons! Screams?

He must have read our body language because he yelled out, 'I'm friendly.'

We felt foolish and I suspect he felt guilty because he kept talk-yelling to us as he approached, explaining himself and his reasons for being here. By the time he'd closed the distance between us, we'd learned he was an occasional worker for Mum and knew Mary's husband, and that he wasn't going to slaughter us and cut us into tiny pieces so we'd fit in the trench with the decaying sheep.

'G'day,' I said, extending a hand, as if we'd picked him for a good bloke the moment we saw him in the black hat, up the Hill, blocking our exit while whistling kites circled.

I can't remember the reason he gave for his visit. I don't remember his name, although I remember him saying a name. I was too focused on scanning his body for a hidden weapon. He didn't stay long and never came back.

❦

We read the landscape through our psyche. And often the translation is muddied by anxiety, sadness, optimism or the stories we've just told ourselves. I might feel calm jostling against other bodies on buses, or nipping in and out of traffic, or sitting within elbow room of others in cafes or weaving around walkers along crowded pavements, but the space of the country can feel giddying. The terror of the terroir.

It takes a while for a city person to feel at ease in the expanse of the country, to feel as if they belong there, to take the temperature and know what's coming, to scan the landscape and not see a horror story. If I breathe in a little deeper and breathe out slower, my body becomes easier in the new terrain and less of a target for its terrors. But at night I can still hear that refrain, 'Bloody bones in the woodshed!', and my mind leaps to the dead sheep in the ditch.

5

Old Enough to Know Better

M y sister Wendy and Roger and I are meeting another winegrowing couple at the local wine bar. 'They're exactly like you,' says Wendy. 'They have a small vineyard about twenty kilometres from your place, a couple of different varieties of grapes and they've contracted out the wine-making. They're retiring now, so you might be able to buy their nets cheaply.'

It's that word 'retire' that plants the image of the couple we are due to meet. Old, chiselled, barely ambulant on knees that should have been replaced decades ago. Straw hanging out their mouths. Battle-scarred hands.

Tony and Deb bound into the wine bar with their teenage daughter. We register each other with surprise. My surprise goes like this: *Oh my God, they are ten or fifteen years younger than us! Why are they retiring from wine growing?*

Their surprise looks something like this: *Oh my God, they must be ten or fifteen years older than us; what are they doing starting a vineyard?'*

It isn't the first time that our age has been noted. A few months ago, when Roger was at the local wine bar talking with a couple of irrigators and winemakers, one of the tipsy blokes listens to Roger's plan and pipes up, 'How old are you?'

There is so much meta behind that question. In the workforce, in sport, in fashion, in hobbies or holiday choices, that question is really a statement, and it means one thing: 'You're too old for that.' And there's another subtext that goes: 'Why do you think you can do that, when others don't? It's like they feel you're making a judgement on their choices.

The concept of age-appropriateness dogs our endeavours and the reminders come from both locals and friends. Some of it is concern for our welfare, but some of these comments suggest that we have no idea of what we're getting ourselves into and that our ignorance will be our downfall. We're not feeling confident in ourselves, especially when we climb up into the cranky tractor, so we don't need to be reminded of our foolhardiness.

Still, in wine-growing circles the question of age has some pertinence. After all, it takes years for vines to produce grapes worthy of turning into wine. Roger says it takes three years. I say five or six years, but then I'm eight years younger than him and I have a few more vintages in my actuarial table. When we planted our first vines, I was sixty and Roger was sixty-eight years, so we might be drinking our first vintage when I'm sixty-five and Roger is seventy-three. Any earlier and we'll be sprinkling it on salads.

Leaving aside the importance of being alive to taste the first vintage, and having tastebuds to appreciate it, there is the question of the sort of work required in a vineyard. It taxes the age-disadvantaged. Even with help from machinery and local labour, there are days (really months) of bending, crouching, stretching, tying, cutting, carting, feeding, mowing, spraying and lifting. And most of this work takes place in summer, when temperatures can reach 40 degrees. Its only resemblance to gardening is that there are refreshments afterwards.

In rural areas, it's not unusual to see old people with knees in need of a surgeon or hips that tilt bodies at painful angles. The average age of the Australian farmer is fifty-six.

That's the oldest workforce in the country. And younger than Roger and me.

But we're not alone. Our generation—yes, baby boomers—doesn't approach retirement with much grace. Some love it, but I suspect those who can embrace the leisured years have more grace, imagination or better fishing spots. Or really dodgy knees. For those who think work is better than sex, retirement is worse than death. But, if there aren't that many jobs for those with a CV beginning in 1974, then you just create your own job.

Reinvention at any age is exciting, but it's poignant at our age. When you've done your career, you're free to choose your love. And even if your career was your love, there are other loves you probably left behind when your mother's warning—you'll end up a garbo—convinced you to start studying.

The careers we bypassed are often our romantic personas. They are dreams of us as painters, writers, gardeners, philosophers, photographers or farmers. They are us as creators of gadgets, designers of greeting cards or travel guides to the opera houses of Europe. The late-life romantics buy the villa in Spain and put up a B&B shingle. And they do it not to make a fortune or a reputation but to remake themselves into someone they might have always been.

The second-life career often looks enticing for those still wearing suits into town. It sounds irrational to those who measure life against a ledger. It annoys the hell out of those who want life to follow an orderly and predictable sequence. But fuck it. When you decide to start on a project that speaks to your heart, when you hear the call of another self, it's liberating. You've escaped the cage of your age. You've heard the nay-sayers and decided you're still going to do it.

We pick up lots of tips from the couple in the wine bar. They've had fifteen years in wine growing, lots of disasters, one gold medal and a deep respect for downy mildew. We might yet buy their nets, even though they are damaged by kangaroo hits and hold the remains of a few snakes. But we're in no rush. The poles and wires of the vineyard are in place; the grow line, where we will be planting, has been ploughed and the irrigation pipes have been strung along the bottom wires. We're ready to plant a vineyard, but we are years away from needing nets.

Part of me is hoping that technology will have found something better by the time we need to protect our first vintage. Even though our vineyard is yet to see a single vine, I'm hoping that I don't have to wrestle kilometres of

6

Pumped for Planting

The vines arrive on a hot day in late October. The 1300 shiraz and sangiovese rootlings are crammed into two crates. I peer into their cradles and panic. The vines are just stems in biodegradable paper wrappings. They look like a sneeze would shred them, and yet they have to be pulled from the crates and planted into holes in the dusty rows of the vineyard and then cope with whatever the weather throws at them.

When the truck driver, having delivered the two pallets holding our future vineyard, starts driving away, I feel like calling out to him and saying, 'Take them back! We're bound to kill them!' It's like taking your first-born home from hospital. You can't believe they're leaving you in charge of the baby.

The rootlings spend the next few days in their crates as we wait for family and friends to gather for the planting days. I visit them morning and evening with a long hose and spray a mist over their foliage—not so much of it that they get their paper wrappings sodden but enough to keep their roots cool. Snug in the two crates, they look promising. But I can't help looking around the crates for planting instructions.

On the first day of planting, we muster four field labourers—Roger and me, and my sisters Mary and Wendy —and we start by having an argument.

'You need to plant them 30 centimetres deep with 10 centimetres of soil covering the top of the paper wrapping,' Roger tells us.

'That sounds too deep. Plants rot if you cover their stems too high with soil,' I say.

Roger has studied planting methods online, in books, in pamphlets and with anyone he knows who has ever been involved with vines. He is right. I am wrong, but I am nervous and don't want to kill these plants before they have a chance to grow taller than their paper cases.

The first dozen vines take an hour to plant. We all continue to debate depth of planting, distance from the irrigation line, whether the vines have a face-out side, how much fertiliser to drop into the hole, how wide to make the hole, whether to add water before or after planting, and how to put the vine guard around the plant. The vine guards alone are difficult. They are half-a-metre-tall fibreboards that are folded around the little trunks and zipped closed. It shouldn't be complicated, but it is when it's all new and the labourers are nervous and it's getting hotter as the arguments continue. It's also important because the vines will be in the ground, exactly where you put them, a hundred years from now.

I become acutely aware of how much time it is taking. If twelve vines have taken four people an hour to plant, then 1300 vines would take more than one hundred hours. At eight hours of work a day, that would mean it would be twelve and a half days before the last vine is planted—or the last twig, because these baby vines wouldn't survive that long in their cradles. (Okay, they might survive, but the planting guide says they should be in the ground within days.)

I step up the pace. And that's never good news for others. I am curt in my instructions, quick to pick mistakes and so determined to get these plants in the ground that I don't stop for a chat, take a deep breath or a drink water. By the time a break is called (by the others) I am dizzy and prone under a tree.

'Heat exhaustion?' asks Wendy, staring down at me as I pale under the shade of the tree.

'No, just heat stress I think,' says Mum, who's arrived with sandwiches.

Even as I lie in the shade, hoping that my heart isn't about to reveal an overlooked weakness, I am cursing the lost time. *Get up, you lazy sod, there's soooo much work to do.* The others are flaked out under trees and probably wondering what the hell they are doing here when they could be back on their own bits of country, feeding horses or watching sheep pass or swishing around the garden in a floral dress.

We are all old-ish. I am the youngest at sixty, for God's sake. We haven't laboured in a field since . . . ever. We are fit enough to plunge into a pool or skip up a few steps to the local gym, but we aren't field fit. Peasant fit.

I suck on water bottles for about an hour, trying to think of a better strategy. The idea of peasant fitness plays on my mind. Those farm workers I'd spotted outside when on swift train rides through Europe had been old and not that fit, judging by the cigarettes dangling from their mouths. Sure, they were slow—but maybe they were just pacing themselves. Work early, break often, finish before the sun turns mean; chat, drink and plod on.

I know I should drop the managerial outcomes approach to the land; leave the city mentality behind when the highway turns from suburbia to bushland. I should submit to the centuries-old pace of peasants and learn to work with whatever nature has delivered that day. Maybe I also have to face the reality of sixty years on this planet.

By the time the weekend arrives, we have a third of the vineyard planted and two of my children and their partners, plus my brother-in-law and nephew arrive to help. For the next two days we have eight to nine peasants and I've anointed myself supervisor, not because I want to avoid hard work but because I'm good with logistics and, okay, I'm naturally bossy. I'm in charge of ensuring that every peasant has enough vines, watering cans, weather shields, clips, gloves, water supplies and holes dug ahead of them. I ensure they rotate jobs so they won't get repetition injuries or complain of boredom. I am consultant for their queries when Roger isn't around. I arrange breaks, lunch, sometimes jokes, and I try really hard not to be bossy.

If the kids are surprised at how much work we're inveigling them into on their weekend in the country, they are too kind to say. None of us is getting paid, some of us are out of pocket (now that is a real boss achievement, although the boss isn't being paid either). We work, drink beers, hoe into hamburgers, slip around on mud during showers, swap hats for rain jackets and tell jokes about the bossy supervisor.

And still many of the rows stretch ahead of us, awaiting their residents.

By the time our weekend labourers leave on the Sunday afternoon, there are two long rows left. And I am feeling the deadline pressure again. The baby vines still in the crates, although sprayed regularly, are wilting. My kids must leave. Then my sisters have to go and, as the sun tilts to the west, I have to leave for work in Sydney. On Monday Roger, my brother-in-law and my nephew remain to tackle the last two rows.

As I drive away from the Hill and stare back at the vineyard in the rearview mirror, I see hard work. And the efforts of a lovely bunch of people. I salute the power of imagination that first appeared on that walk around the rubbishy hill a year ago and has resulted in a vineyard.

But mostly I see Arlington Cemetery. More than a thousand vines are encased in their white shields and standing sentinel over the Hill. So straight (well, mostly straight). So proud looking. They are doing a good job of mimicking the world's most impressive military cemetery. Perhaps not the best of images.

I try not to dwell on it. I won't let myself believe that our amateur enthusiasm may result in a mass grave. The folly of war cannot be our fate.

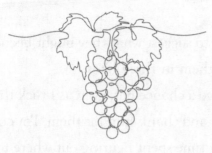

7

Stick by Stick

Every few weeks, my brother-in-law Stefan helps at the Landcare market stall, where tiny saplings are sold to passers-by to help revegetate the country. Sometimes the sight of those twigs makes me laugh—a trestle table of twigs is supposed to help reforest a continent? At other times, I feel like crying at the idea that community stalls selling saplings are the most visible endeavour of a country repairing two centuries of land clearing. Sisyphus comes to mind and not just because of the rocks on our Hill.

Today Stefan hands to me a couple of unsold saplings he has rescued from the market table. The word 'sapling' gives them a status beyond their maturity. I think they are snow gums, but they are such tiny sticks they barely have enough leaves to suggest what they might become. A locust could devour them in three bites.

They deserve a chance but, even as I tuck the $1 saplings under my arm and thank him for them, I'm counting their true cost—the time spent figuring out where to plant them and the effort spent keeping them alive until their roots are deep enough. They can't go in the sheep paddocks, because they wouldn't last a day of grazing and, even if they had a cage of chicken wire surrounding them, you would barely see them for the blades of grass. They could go somewhere in the vineyard area, but not too close to the vines, not under electricity wires, not near established trees, nor near car turning-circles. And they can't be planted in sight lines that would block views when they reach maturity in the twenty-second century. After writing off all the negative spaces, I search for spaces where these twigs/future trees would enhance the outlook, hide the banal, complement the contours of the land and save the planet.

I'm making this up as I go, wandering around the vineyard with saplings tucked to my chest, imaging the future of these dozen sticks. It strikes me as naively ambitious and vaguely artistic. I am defining the landscape with trees, colouring its brown scalp with foliage, adding movement to the wind.

Dab, dab, dab. Eventually I decide to plant them along a fence. I know that their branches may fall on the fence in thirty years' time but I'm getting impatient, because already I know what these twigs will demand. This land is getting dry, showers are less frequent and, if the drought in the north-west of the country edges down this way, these twigs will be cactus.

When you plant in a dry period, you are nursemaid for at least the first year; already I have seventy-eight new plantings that need hand-watering at least once a week. That's 80 to 100 litres of water carted to various areas and slowly poured around the root circle. Wait ten seconds and pour again. Wait twenty seconds, another pour. Their plastic shields help retain moisture, as do water crystals, but the watering routine in this dry period takes more than an hour.

As I water the snow gum saplings, I imagine how their spindly limbs will determine their future shape. I can see the smooth bark of strong limbs in their pencil shapes and imagine their leaves dancing in the wind. I also wonder whether I'll be around to see them. There's a saying that speaks to this. It's Greek and it goes: 'A society grows great when old men plant trees in whose shade they will never sit.'

I mull on this as I complete my watering. Like many old sayings, the gender tag is annoying. I'll bet many of those trees in ancient Greece were planted by old women. And I'll bet those women would never have had time to sit under them, even if they did live long enough. They'd have been sweeping up leaves as their husbands sat under trees and gossiped. But I get the gist. Obviously, it's a metaphor for the wisdom of investing for future communities, building a future for your grandchildren.

Planting trees is a gift to the next generation. And a gift to the land. In Australia it could be considered reparation for two centuries during which we have regarded the land as nothing more than a factory. It's been a good factory—and hopefully this bit of land will be a good wine factory—but we've taken more than we've given back. The bare peak of the Hill, casting its shadow over my twig plantings, is proof of that. Science tells us that. Farmers, too, are telling us that. But even a visiting city person could figure out that you don't have to denude a plain to get grazing pasture.

So, I plant for the landscape, but I'm not planting to give the next generation a shady place to sit. I want to stand under the trees. I want to admire them. Welcome them back to the land. Hug them even.

I've started buying bigger trees. They are about a year old and I surround them with plastic sleeves held in place by bamboo stakes. I plant companion trees nearby and visit often to check on progress. Not that I stand over them, drumming my fingers while they do their best to fulfil the potential on the labels, but I whooped when I read recently that most native trees achieve 60 per cent of their lifetime growth in their first decade. I have a chance of being there for their adulthood.

Like most of what we are doing on the farm, I'm learning as we go. Or, more precisely, learning after I've done it. Bung in a plant and then think: *Ummm, maybe I should know more about this variety.* Or bung a tree along the driveway and realise I haven't checked how far its branches will spread.

My biggest concern is whether I'm planting in the right area. I have swathes of trees—that's such a city garden idea—and most are in spots where I think a swathe would look good. But is that where the landscape needs them? Does nature plant itself in clumps, in swathes? Or just wherever it can get a toehold? After two centuries of mucking around with the natural vegetation of this continent, do we even know how gum trees like to grow?

I have read books on this. Two of the most recent books are about the secret life of trees. Evidently, trees are companionable; they like living in communities, where they can support each other. They swap nutrients via fungi in the soil, and some say they communicate with each other, via fungi or by emitting chemicals into the air.

My favourite story on talkative trees is the one about how trees in Africa's savannah can alert other trees to grazing giraffes. So, even as trees are being devoured by giraffes, they are emitting a warning signal to trees further away. When trees further away get a whiff of this warning, they begin secreting chemicals that giraffes don't find tasty. It sounds a bit like James Bond in the service of botany.

I like the idea of building a community of trees. As long as they all get along with each other. It would be awful to plonk a tree in a community and then discover that the others couldn't abide it. You'd just be planting orphans.

The other book that guides me as I attempt to create a society of saplings—in a pleasing swathe pattern—is Charles Massy's *Call of the Reed Warbler*. A farmer in the Monaro area about 100 kilometres south of Cockatoo Hill, Massy taught himself to read the Australian landscape, to listen to its needs, to watch when it fails and when it flourishes. Most importantly, he talked to other farmers who had rescued their lands from poor farming practices and, in the process, rescued their farms. One of his most urgent messages in his books is that we must revegetate the land, and one of his major suggestions is that replanting should start at the top of hills.

The scalp of our Hill haunts me because of its rocky loneliness, but revegetating it would be a nightmare. I would have to drag hundreds of saplings up the Hill and surround them with star pickets and chicken wire to protect them from the sheep. I'd need to haul megalitres of water up the Hill to keep them alive in a drought. And, if I did, half of them would still fail and the Hill might just end up looking like it was pocked with hair plugs.

Some agriculture agencies, like Landcare, suggest corridor planting or group planting. Some trees don't like being alone, and not just because they feel lonely. Wildlife needs nature corridors. Soil and water systems can repair under good planting systems. So too can micro-climates. Corridors of nature make sense too because farmers can fence around corridors, sparing the saplings—twigs—from the appetites of livestock.

I get the gist, but I should be more educated in this. Shouldn't there be a textbook for this? Shouldn't there be guidance from governments or science bodies on this? This is meant to be a national emergency and yet people like me are faffing around with $1 twigs, wondering if we're doing it right and whether it will look pretty.

I have time to get cranky about this on my watering rounds. Are my efforts of reparation stupid? Misplaced? Useless? Will they just be pretty? And those other farmers who care for the land, who care for it as a piece of the planet and not just a property, are they doing the right thing? If we really want people to look after the land, shouldn't we help them do that with education, guidance, even cheap plants? I have asked organisations for educational material or a place where I can source good ideas or appropriate plants. They politely say they don't have the resources, and sometimes they name the year and the government that suspended their funding.

Down on the farm, you can hear the chants from the city that the land must be saved. And so it must. But it won't be done with chants. It can partly be done by carting loads of water and dribbling the water over twiggy infants, watching the moisture soak into the dust and imagining the roots reaching out for a drink and the limbs reaching for the sky. But it would more sensibly be done by a community that is prepared to back its chants with money, muscle, policies and politicians.

A few days later, I revisit the saplings that Stefan gifted us. Only two have survived. One was dug up, presumably by rabbits, although there could be other pests here that I haven't encountered. One got flattened by a limb off an old gum—obviously it was too close to the old fella. Two others seem to have disappeared and I wonder about them. The wind? Rabbits again? A hungry locust? Surely, the $1 twigs aren't worth stealing.

I scuff dirt into the holes that rabbits left when they dug up the saplings and see that the soil is powdery dry. There is no sign of the watering I'd done a few days ago. Not even dampness. Maybe the twigs could sense they had no future here on this land, in this year when the rains are less frequent and the creeks are getting sluggish. Is it even fair to plant rootlings at a time when soils are turning dusty and talk around town is all about the dry?

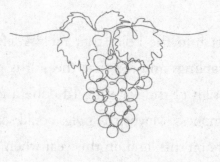

8

Hard Graft

A couple of months after planting the vineyard, the tips of the vines are waving at us from above the vine guards. Some are still shy of the guard, some are peeking their tips above the guard, but others have leapt free and are swaying in the breeze.

Waving or drowning? I'm getting nervous about what we need to do next in the vineyard, but Roger is feeling good about it, having read a few books and articles and watched a few videos. Evidently YouTube is so full of training videos that you could build a house on the back of a few video tutorials.

I'm not so confident the University of YouTube can solve all our problems. It seems there's still a lot we should know about how to get these happy tips peeking out of their shields up to the wire, settled along the wire, growing in the correct shape on the wire and—dah, dah!—producing grapes. Then we have a serendipitous moment.

Having tasted a particularly nice pinot noir at the local wine bar—the only wine bar in town—I tell Roger I'm going to order a dozen from the winery. I call the number given on the vineyard's website and begin placing the order. It's a habit of city people to assume that, when you make such a call, you are talking to a call-centre worker located anywhere in Australia, or in South Africa, India or the Philippines.

The person on the end of the phone (he sounds Australian) finishes taking my details and asks, 'Where do you want it delivered?' I reply that I normally live in Sydney, but I am actually in the country today. Country? Yes, outside Canberra. He then says he could drop it off to our property because he is working in a vineyard nearby today.

Working in a vineyard? Nearby? What's with that?

Richard explains that he has his own vineyard 200-odd kilometres away, but that he also manages a vineyard down the highway from us and is in fact the former president of the local wine industry organisation.

'You're exactly the person we need,' I declare.

A week later, Richard was in the vineyard and we had our first on-site tutorial and a consultant viticulturist on our contacts list.

Training vines is a bit like toilet training a toddler. It's hard to know when to begin, it's messy, you don't want to do anything that might create lasting trauma and it's easy to end up crying with frustration.

Here's the gist. When the vine has shot past the guard and is waving at you from above the grow wire, you inspect it to see if it's ready for training. Ideally, the main shoot—and future trunk—should be pencil thickness before you tackle it (mostly we are too impatient and start when it's the thickness of a fine paint brush). Before you cut the top off the main shoot, you check to see if the buds below it are in the right position. One of them should be a few inches down the stem so it can sprout a branch to the right side of the trunk; the other should be a few inches under that, so it can be directed to the left side. The lower bud should be no more than a hand length below the grow wire.

The idea is that you want a trunk with an asymmetrical V at the top, so the two branches can be grown on either side of the grow line. If all this is aligned—and it rarely is—you cut the main vine through the bud, leaving a bulge so you can loop a twine over it and attach the twine to the grow wire. This little nub thing will help the trunk to grow straight and hold the vine in place until it is too old and gnarly to move.

Roger and I struggled from the start. We couldn't get the knots right—one should be a slip knot and the other a double half-hitch knot—but we were never in the Scouts, we didn't go camping as kids and Bear Grylls wasn't on TV when we were young, so we were all thumbs. Richard taught us both knots again. And then again. He was polite, even though he had a baffled look on his face that suggested the thought, *How can these people not get this?*

Part of the early training also requires stripping the random growths from the bottom of the vine, because these take vigour from the main branch, which is where you want the action to happen. This involves unzipping the guards, cutting off the suckers and zipping up the guards. Roger and I struggled with zipping the guards.

Richard was patient, but after about half an hour, when we had only managed to train about half-a-dozen vines, he did the maths. If six vines took us half an hour, then by the time we'd trained 1300 vines—roughly three working weeks—it would be time to start again because those first vines would be in need of more training. These babies grow 3 centimetres a day in spring so if you don't keep up with them your vineyard will resemble a platoon of triffids. Richard said he knew two young women who were keen to practise their viticultural skills and would be prepared to work the odd day in the vineyard. Richard was sent from God. From Bacchus, at least.

Brooke and Chrissie arrived the next week and they didn't look like field workers. Brooke and her husband run the local restaurant and raise two children, and Chrissie is studying viticulture and runs events and does tech work for local businesses and is basically talented in many ways that have nothing to do with tractors. They both have perfect complexions, so I guessed they didn't ride around paddocks on quad bikes too often. They were adding to their skill sets (city talk) but, as we worked alongside one another in the spring sunshine over the next few weeks, I came to realise that this was an escape for them too. Away from children, demanding diners and clients, you can enter into a meditation with the vines. Each vine presents a puzzle to be solved, a future to be shaped, a work with nature and of nature. And the only noisy gangs you hear are galahs.

They went on to work with us for the next few years, mainly in the fast-growing season between October and Christmas, and Richard stayed for the duration, advising us on equipment, spraying, soils, seminars and contacts. Richard would also eventually introduce us to a winemaker.

I really don't know how we could have coped if we had had to grow a vineyard from YouTube videos. We wouldn't have coped without the labour of those cheerful and hard-working locals. If not for Richard, I would still be using secateurs that were way too big for me. I doubt the trunks would be straight (Richard is a stickler for straight trunks) and I never would have learned that if a black snake passes nearby, you shouldn't jump into the air, yelp and run in the other direction. You just stand still. Yeah.

But, most importantly, we might never have been introduced to the wine-growing fraternity of the area. So much of surviving and thriving in the country depends on who you know. Not just who you know but whether they like knowing you. We lucked into a circle of great knowledge, goodwill and contacts. And I don't know if we deserved that, coming from the city with YouTube training, economic thinking and an urban ignorance of the value of community.

9

Winded

I was talking on the phone to a friend when the storm arrived. It came from the south-west and swept up to rattle the windows and bang on the door, like a visit from the constabulary. It brought rain and wind and, judging by the sound on the roof, hail.

The rain looked promising. The hail less so. But it was the wind that weirded me out. I was used to Sydney's southerly busters, which arrived with a bang but faded within ten minutes. This wind was sounding meaner by the minute. This wind was different.

'I'd better go,' I said to my friend. 'This is getting serious.' I stood away from the windows and shifted under a doorway and started filming.

Why do we film these things? I'm not an Insta person, but I had recently started pulling out my phone and taking photos or videos of things I didn't understand, stuff I needed to research later or things that would freak out my city friends. It was only when I watched the storm as it was happening on the phone that I noticed the rain was now horizontal and hitting the windows like bullets. I also noticed that I could barely hear anything above the roar of the storm.

Earlier, Roger had said he was going out to the shed to sort tools, and that wasn't the best place to be. The shed was a ramshackle collection of iron sheets nailed up to a dead tree and two old poles. Tyres kept its roof on and habit kept its walls upright. I didn't like its chances of withstanding a stiff south-westerly, much less this event.

But the house didn't seem like much protection either. The rain, hail and wind combined were as loud as a train in a tunnel as they assaulted the roof and walls and windows. I don't think the house was moving, but I could feel the pressure of the wind gusts striking and wondered what would give first. Probably the windows, which were thin and held in place by brittle frames. But it could be the roof. Isn't that what happens in tropical storms? The roof lifts off and cartwheels across the neighbourhood? But the walls might after all prove to be the weakest link as the nails fastening their fibro sheets were already halfway to freedom.

I shifted to the bedroom and looked to the east. It was just as frightening. Especially the tree thrashing around in distress just outside the window. I moved to stand under the bathroom door jamb and realised that there really wasn't a safe place in this old shack. As I crouched within the door frame, I wondered where my body would be found when the rescue crews arrived. Would people say I was stupid to be cowering in the bathroom? Would they say I should have hidden under the bed or the dining table instead? What would they say at my funeral?

Just as the wind eased, Roger walked in from the other side of the house. 'I thought it was protected on the other side, but then the wind started picking up there,' he said. He had spent the early part of the storm in the buggy, snugged up against the northern side of the old house.

Now the wind was coming back. Coming from the other direction. We watched it intently as it returned, wondering what was going to give. I couldn't talk and didn't move, my breathing was light and I think the hairs on my body were standing up. I scanned the ceiling for new cracks, the windows for bowing, the door for weakness.

I felt an unbearable urge to do something. To know what to do. Water in buckets? Blankets on heads? Call for help?

And all the time, I'm thinking it would be embarrassing to be found dead in the wrong part of the house.

The wind eased suddenly and then disappeared completely. We stood still, just breathing in and out for a while, as if to reassure ourselves that it wasn't going to return. Then we ventured outside. A giant fir tree that normally stood in the corner of the garden was splayed just outside the door. It had split halfway up its trunk in a corkscrew movement and looked like it had been wrung by a giant. It must have made a huge noise when it cracked and crashed to the ground, but, such was the noise of the storm, I hadn't heard it. Its crown was a metre from the back door.

We walked around the property. A giant elm tree was split down the middle of its trunk but was still standing. Smaller wattles had been beheaded cleanly; their trunks too looked like a corkscrew. Then we saw the collapsed hay shed further up the Hill. The ironbark poles had shattered from their concrete footings; the new tractor was entombed by roofing iron.

We didn't want to inspect the vineyard, afraid of what we'd find. If the storm had shredded a century-old fir with a trunk so thick that two hippies couldn't hug it, then what had it done to the tender rootlings just emerging from their shields? We made our way to the vineyard in silence. Every vine that had shot out of its vine guard was damaged. The tender tips were sheared off, leaves torn. Many shields had been uprooted and tossed around the vineyard, like discarded tissues.

It was fortunate that many vines were still encased within their shields. They suffered only minor damage. I guess we were fortunate that the whole vineyard was so young. No fruit to lose, no mature growth damaged.

We wondered whether this was normal. Is this the country equivalent of a southerly buster?

The next day a neighbour from up the valley dropped by to see how we'd fared. She said that other neighbours had been caught in the field and rushed to a shed, getting bruised by hail along the way, and then the door to the shed had blown off in front of them. Another neighbour discovered that all their equipment inside a new shed had been swept out the door. Everywhere, horses had been spooked and many old sheds were down. Then, a few days later, we saw in the local paper a photo of the storm taken by a volunteer firefighter, who was just over our Hill when the storm hit. The photo showed the dark funnel of a tornado.

'I hope you're not in a tornado-prone spot,' our viticulturalist Richard said when we phoned him and asked him to inspect the damage. I looked up at the Hill and wondered if those dead trees and fallen trunks were the result of past tornados. There is so much about this land we don't know—the local weather patterns, the history of its weather—and so much we can't know with climate change.

Our first summer was a tough introduction to the land. We experienced more storms; some were big enough to take down old trees in the paddock and toss their limbs around the house. We had hail damage to the shoots that replaced the tornado-damaged shoots. We had locusts, although their appetite wasn't too great. We arrived one day to find water streaming from the ceiling in the old part of the house—on the very weekend we were accompanied by our kids and were expecting to have a fun time. We had sheep escape their paddocks and enter the vineyard, chewing every bit of green growth they could reach. And all through that season, the periods between rainfalls lengthened and the amount of rainfall grew lighter.

We repaired the vines more often than we trained them. I continued to plant trees even though I wondered whether I was setting them up for a tough life or a brief one. It got to the point where we would arrive at the property full of apprehension at what might have happened in our absence.

We'd joke about it with Sydney friends—the quiet life in the country—but locals just shrugged. To them, out of the normal was normal.

It's easy to feel cursed by nature in the country. Droughts and flooding rains, etc. City solutions to hardship or failure are all about moving on, finding something new, cutting your losses early. It seems strange, maybe even stupid, to keep plugging away at something that causes such regular grief. City Deirdre had always wondered why those country people who were caught in droughts, floods, debt, losses and diseases didn't just move to the city and get a job. You can feel both admiration and exasperation for country people.

That tough summer gave me a hint as to why there are still people prepared to work in the country. There's pig-headedness—an unwillingness to be defeated by an event—and a tradition, a history really, of rising to the challenges of the land. There might also be a sense of not knowing what else to do, especially for people like Ian; he has such deep expertise in everything to do with the land, but nothing that he could put on a fridge magnet for city clients.

But I think there's also a feeling of acceptance. After a while, after so many adverse events, you must reach a point where you think: this is life. This is normal. This is what happens here. Knowing that disasters happen routinely doesn't take away the severity of the disaster, but it does take away the stress of fretting about it.

I'd like to think that one day I'll be able to cut up twisted and fallen trees without cursing the weather. Or retrain damaged vines without feeling resentment at the wind. Or rebuild sheds without counting the loss. Or tell city friends of the latest disaster without feeling like a fool.

But people have their limits. I'm not sure when I'll meet my limit, or what I'll do. It takes something really big to shift most people off their land, out of their livelihood, away from their heritage. It might not take that much to shift me.

That summer wasn't just a series of small disasters; the Bureau of Meteorology (BOM) was tracking a 'severe deficiency' in rainfall. Farmers were already de-stocking in ahead of it. The dams were rimmed with pancakes of brown, cracked dirt, even if they still had a dirty sludge at the base. The ground that we had slithered around on when we were planting in the rain was becoming concrete. The drying of this land would put all the other challenges into the just-normal basket.

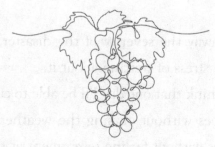

10

Back to School for a Continent

It's 9 am. Weak winter sun, 2 degrees with a wind chill. We arrive at the Mulloon Institute farm, which nestles in a valley to the north of the ACT and is worked as a model for regenerative farming. Passing groves of recently planted trees (many European varieties, what's with that?) my sister Mary and brother-in-law Stefan and I reach a converted shed. About a hundred people have booked for a landscape resilience forum, to hear how farmers, academics and scientists are building sustainable landscapes in an age of climate change.

The gathering is diverse. Many are older farmers, their complexions as weathered as their hats. Others look more like urban farmers—a bit more polish on the boot.

There are also several people with ensigns of government departments on their vests. This is great, they've come to hear what locals are doing to save their environments. Briefly I wonder why these taxpayer-funded experts haven't got the answers already. Isn't it a tradition that government scientists discover the best way to do things and then inform farmers about it? Shouldn't there be scientific papers on this? An information service for farm problems?

Later in the conference, Peter Andrews, the gruff pioneer of water management systems in a drought-blighted land, refers to this. 'We can't all make ourselves experts on this. What we need is an advisory service. We pick up the phone and ask for expert help when the car breaks down, why can't we do that when the land breaks down?' And he's an expert.

In the absence of a government hot line, the Mulloon Institute has become a gathering place for farmers wanting to rescue their land from drought, chemical toxicity and a century or two of mostly unsustainable farming practices. It began a decade ago when the owner of this land, Tony Coote, took Peter Andrews along his 3-kilometre creek and asked him what to do. The farm now showcases some of the management tools for caring for land and the institute takes the message to wider audiences—working across 23,000 hectares, 50 kilometres of creek, 7000 landholders and a few states.

It's a network, a country-wide web of farmers who share their stories. On this winter's day, huddling around heaters and stomping our boots on the ground to get blood circulating again, we hear some of the stories.

There is David Marsh of Allendale Farm north of Yass, who came from a typical farming background of 'riding the roller-coaster from euphoria to despair'. His wake-up call came with two events—the 1982 drought, which reduced his land to a moonscape, and the death of his twenty-year-old son. The photo he shows of his property in 1982 is shocking and he says he still feels shame showing it today. He tells us his family had become physically sick because of the chemicals they had been using on the land, but that they couldn't see how to do it differently. In desperation, he experimented with holistic management of land, letting the land rest, planting trees.

He now describes himself as a manager of the land: 'We manage sunlight, plants and time.' This sounds different to most stories of farming we've heard through the years. I thought farmers managed livestock and maybe water. But manage sunlight? Time?

His story is followed by that of Gillian Sanbrook, an elegant, middle-aged farmer from Bowna, 130 kilometres south of Wagga Wagga. When she bought her property in 2007, it was degraded, over-grazed, full of rabbits and weeds, and covered with gully erosion and soils so depleted that, when it rained, the water and the remaining soil fertility flowed straight off the land. She then fenced the gullies to prevent livestock from entering the waterways, she tripled the number of paddocks to rotate livestock through pastures and she planted 60,000 trees (she was lucky to have done the work in 2008 when the federal government began the program aimed at planting a million trees). She tells the seminar it's time to take the 'hope' out of farming, conjuring up that cliché image of a farmer sitting on the verandah hoping for rain. She too talks of managing the land, not managing stock, because if your land isn't managed you can't manage stock. She says her way of operating now is to ask herself: 'How do we want this property to look in a hundred years?'

The speakers here see the landscape in a different way— different to the way I'd envisaged but also different to the old textbooks on farming. Many quote Peter Andrews and Charles Massy—their experiences and theories. They seem to have a gut understanding of what the land needs. They read it, perhaps like the traditional custodians read the land. Is this a form of empathy? Or a seventh sense? Seeing the way water wants to move across the land, seeing the paths of animals—native and livestock—and drawing lessons from them. Hearing the sounds of the land and understanding what they're hearing. Sniff it. Taste it. Know how it's changing, even from day to day.

Hear the call of the land. That is the message of the day. These innovative farmers—using methods they've largely discovered themselves through trial and error and keeping an ear out for the land—prioritise the land first and the production second. If the pasture isn't ready for livestock, they don't stock. Or they de-stock.

Farmers used to say, 'I must do everything to save my livestock'; these farmers say, 'I must do everything to save my soil.' Some are brutal about it. Gillian trades livestock and only carries them on the land if the land is ready. If not, hey, she travels (okay, she's probably pretty rich). There is no set stocking here. There's landscape and even that's not set. It's cared for, it's developed, it's enriched. And, if they do it right, it then enriches them.

These aren't hippies, tying up the land for eternity or reserving it for wildlife. They say, 'You can't be green if you're in the red.' And most of them have made their farms more profitable, even after they've devoted a quarter of their land to trees, even after they've fenced off creeks or increased their paddocks from seven to seventy.

The global markets are moving with them. More consumers want produce that comes from sustainable farms, from environmentally focused producers, from clean and green fields. They want meals to be moral. They won't sacrifice the health of the land for the sake of a steak. Farming is being fashioned from afar.

❦

We leave late in the day. It's still only 6 degrees and the wind is fresh off the Snowy Mountains. We pass the groves of trees and now know the deciduous trees were chosen because the fallen leaves will help build the soil and slow the bushfires. We pass the leaky dams, which capture and slow down water so it can seep into the surrounding ground. We pass the many paddocks that enable livestock to graze richly and then move onto paddocks that have been rested and replenished for several months. We leave behind the sounds of roosters, guinea hens, peacocks, ducks and horses.

This farm, stretching along a gentle valley, feels calm, even during drought. Maybe it's the afternoon light or the inspiring stories, but it feels like a sanctuary.

And then I think of Cockatoo Hill. And my attempts at planting swathes of trees from two-leaf saplings: spading out thistle and feeling totally inadequate when I look at the soil, wondering if has been leached of life. Will the Hill ever look or feel this well cared for? And have I done the right thing planting natives?

I feel ignorant, but then those government officers with ensigns on their chests are too. And those farmers attending the seminar don't have all the answers either. We're less ignorant than we were this morning, but I hope we can get onto a fast-learning curve, because I'm not sure the land can wait.

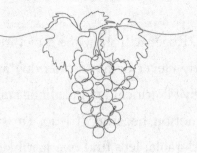

11

An Imaginary Friend

'We have a new pet at the farm.' Roger looks at me, gauging my reaction. I pause for a bit to work out the puzzle.

We're in Sydney, so there probably isn't a puppy tied up to the mud room door, gazing up at Cockatoo Hill, wondering if one of the ewes is its mother. But he has just finished a call with Ian, who gave him an update on work he has been doing. Could Ian have given Roger a pup? Has Patrick, who manages the sheep on the property, visited the farm with his dogs and left behind one of their recent offspring? Both Ian and Patrick know Roger wants a dog. Hell, everyone knows it.

The subject of a dog has been kicking around our household for years. It's become a don't-talk-about-the-war topic.

Every so often, Roger will show me a picture on Instagram of a particularly clever or handsome dog and I will have to respond. I give a critical appraisal but am careful not to express any emotion because, if I do, I'm sure Roger will say—yes, it's adorable, let's find one just like it!

I get why he wants a dog. He has seen dogs in the country. You just have to witness dogs in the country to know that it's right. He's seen Patrick and his dogs round up sheep like they are an Olympic team of musterers. There is such skill and communication between the man on the bike and his dogs as they circle a few hundred sheep and steer them towards the small holding pen at the base of the shed. The chorus of whistles, swear words, yaps and bleats bounces off the Hill as Roger and I watch from the kitchen. Dogs leaping on and off the back of the bike, scrambling over the backs of sheep, barely denting the fleece, flying over fences in a single bound. And when the work is done and the sheep are crammed together in the pen and the sun is slipping down the western slope of the Hill, the dogs prowl around the vehicles, or lounge in the shade of the twisted old gum, or mooch up to Roger for a sniff of his extended hand. Barry, the ageing lead dog, is always first to seek a pat.

Even I like Barry. He is one of the older dogs—a kelpie cross—and the most social. When Barry arrives at the farm with Patrick and his compatriots, he's torn between wanting

74

to get out in the fields with the pack and wanting to spend time with humans. You can see it on his face when we're standing in the driveway. The young dogs are always keen to get going; they circle the driveway area, sniffing the air for sheep. If they had a bit, they'd champ it.

Barry keeps an eye on the other dogs, following their focus, ready to jump the fence with them in pursuit of sheep. But he also attends to the humans, angling for a pat, searching our eyes for affection. He's so happy when Roger gives his ears a ruffle.

Recently, Barry had an accident while jumping a fence. He didn't make it. Or at least his hind leg didn't make it. It was torn and stripped of its skin. The vet said it would cost $6000 to fix and no promises about the outcome. Patrick took Barry home, hoping he wouldn't have to find $6000, hoping Barry would mend without the vet's help, hoping he wouldn't have to think about the rifle in his gun safe. Barry recovered. He's such a bright dog that I suspect he knows about the gun safe that's opened whenever an animal sickens.

I get it, too, that Roger wants a dog when he's at the farm by himself. He is there more often than I and he gets lonely. The companionship of dogs is precious to those who are alone. They can trot around the fields with you, chase rabbits, throw themselves at low-flying birds, leap into the cabin of a ute with you, curl around you at night in front of the wood burner, eat the crumbs you drop, keep watch at night for mice and things that go bump. A dog in the country is an animal in heaven. They are made for the country and the country makes them.

Tough boots, a felt hat, a kerchief for the neck, a couple of sharp knives, a gun in the safe. Roger has slowly equipped himself for country life. And it's not affectation. You can't accuse him of being all-hat-no-cattle. It's what's needed. He has the whole kit, but he doesn't have a dog. And everyone we know in the country has a dog. Gone country, got dog.

Dogs are bred, traded, sold and swapped down here on a regular basis. They may not be coddled, but they get a cairn above their corpse when they die. How can you argue against a dog in the country?

I'd better put my side of the argument. Fast. Because I am sounding like a bitch even to myself.

A dog that lives happily in the country will not live so happily in the city and a dog that suits the city won't be much chop in the country. We still live between an inner-city home and the country so choosing a dog to suit both places, both lifestyles, is virtually impossible. If Roger gets a dog that likes to leap high fences in a single bound, that feels compelled to round up mobs of animals and is content to spend the night chained to a verandah, that dog isn't going to like its visits to the city. I have a nightmare about a kelpie leaping the fence of the neighbourhood playground and rounding up the toddlers. But there's a worse scenario and that is of a country dog spending its day in a suburban backyard with nothing to leap, nothing to chase and no mates to work with.

A city dog—one that comes with a haircut, clipped nails and a happy/dopey disposition—isn't going to survive long in the country. It will find a snake and decide to have a play with it, it will be cowed by visiting working dogs or it just might die of shame when visitors laugh at it. Except for the odd town woman, I haven't seen anyone in the country with a pretty dog. I suspect owning a dog like that would be a bit like showing up for field work in ballet flats. Or wearing surf shorts to the local pub. Even as I write this, I wonder if there's an unwritten code in the country for acceptable breeds. Show up with a pomeranian, a dachshund, a bichon frise, a shih tzu, or any breed that sounds like it belongs on a takeaway menu, and you'll be laughed out of town.

My second objection is more sensitive. Roger is entering his eighth decade. A puppy, especially a working dog puppy, has lots of energy. It moves fast, runs fast and does lots of stupid things very rapidly. Roger is a chilled guy. He moves a little more slowly than he once did. He doesn't run. And he doesn't do anything rapidly.

What's more, dogs have a habit of living for fifteen-plus years, especially if they're well cared for. This isn't a problem for people who get dogs when they have kids and the dogs grow up with the kids; when the kids finish school and leave home, the dog dies. But if you're already in your seventies when you get a puppy, you're still going to be running after a dog in your eighties and maybe on your ninetieth birthday. You might beat the dog to the grave.

Now all this sounds very calculating, callous maybe, but you have to do the maths. Or I do. I figure if Roger got a dog, then I'd be looking after the dog within about five to seven years; I could be looking after both dog and husband within ten years. I'm happy to look after my husband—I think there was a wedding vow along those lines—but I never signed up to look after a dog as well. I don't want a dog. And I feel mean about it.

There is a third reason and this one took me a while to appreciate (I have been mulling on this for a long time). It dawned on me while I was mentally preparing for a debate with Roger over the dog question. I love the stage of life that I'm at. I love the fact that my kids have grown up and only require the odd home-cooked meal and attentive ear. I'm relieved that I don't have the constant worry of an infirm older parent. I really like the fact that I don't have to clock onto a regular job and answer to a boss. Or feed a mortgage. I don't have to fix a dinner every night if I'm feeling lazy.

I'm free. I can come and go when I like. I can be profligate with my energy, I don't have to answer to anyone or check my movements against the needs of others. That metronome of caring that has tocked at the back of my mind since I had my first child has clocked off. Owning a dog would turn that metronome on again. I'd have a dependant again—one that would ruin my linen lounge.

When I realised that this was a big part of my resistance to owning a dog—the first dog either of us has owned—I wondered why Roger didn't feel the same. Then I remembered a book I had once read on women and their hormones. Evidently, around menopause, women's hormones for caring plummet (I'm not sure what hormones they are, but I'll take a punt and say they're oestrogen). Women's hormonal balance shifts towards the male hormones. This, the author said, explains why marriages break up at that time of life, why women will leave homes and explore other parts of themselves and other parts of the world at that stage of life. It's not that they don't give a toss. They just don't give a big toss. Coincidentally, when men reach middle age, their hormonal balance begins to shift too and—you guessed it—it shifts towards the feminine end of the spectrum. So, less testosterone, more oestrogen and more caring impulses.

That's about the time when they turn to their wife and declare: a dog would be nice.

There's one more nagging thought. The dog question is about a dog, but it's also a metaphor for how Roger and I are viewing our lives. Roger would move to the country tomorrow; I wouldn't. Not yet, maybe not ever. A dog, aka a working dog, would make that move not only more likely but inevitable. I don't want that decision to be made by a dog.

I really, really hope the new pet at the farm isn't a dog.

Roger pauses to stretch out the moment, enjoying the fear in my eyes.

'It's a cat,' he says. 'A wild cat. Ian saw it the other day. It's really big too.'

'So, a feral cat,' I reply. 'Will we shoot it?'

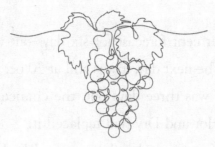

1 2

The Dry

After a while you stop looking for rain. It took me longer than most. Every morning I'd look at the digital horizon—the BOM forecast—and hope to be greeted with good news, but the weather pattern was stuck. Most times I looked, the forecast said hot and dry for the next few days, but often there was a chance of rain in six or seven days. Mostly, it was 20 per cent chance of rain, but sometimes it was as much as a 50 or 60 per cent chance.

The 20 per cent–chance days, you learned to ignore. That would never happen. But you couldn't help feeling hope for the 60 per cent chance. Except. It. Never. Happened.

What would happen is: the next day you'd look up the weather and the 20 per cent–chance day was now No Rain and the 50 per cent forecast for six days out was down to 20 per cent. The next day, it was still at 20 per cent. By the time that day was three days out, the chance of rain had disappeared. Hot and Dry had replaced it.

For most of spring and early summer, I'd relay the BOM report to Mum and my sister if it showed any chance of rain. Yes, Mum would say, but the spring on one of her properties wasn't showing that. Sure, Mary would say, but it never rains if it says 50 or 60 per cent.

Mum's spring intrigued me. It was her personal BOM and mostly, almost always, it was right. Long before a rain event, often two weeks before rain, this spring would begin to flow. If the rain was going to be brief or light, the spring would trickle. If the spring flowed strongly, that indicated a decent rainfall.

Magic? Fairies? Mum wouldn't necessarily argue with that, but she suspected it had more to do with an unknown natural phenomenon, something scientists hadn't picked up but perhaps something the oldest inhabitants of this land might have known about.

I thought it might have something to do with pressure systems—ones that preceded rain by a long time. But I probably only thought that because the idea of air pressure forcing water up through the spring seems a reasonable hypothesis.

All through the spring and early summer, her spring remained dry. And slowly the land dried. The occasional showers, which at least dampened the dust, stopped arriving sometime in October 2019. I'm not sure when the last shower was, but from late October there was no rain. Nor a promise of rain. Nothing on the horizon but blue. Nothing on the BOM but Hot and Dry.

This drought had started further north and west early in 2017, but it had slowly crept down south and east. The nightly news had been telling us what to expect for a year or two. The hardest-hit farms were years into drought now. Their land was pancaked, treeless, cloudless, and their herds had been culled to a few dozen sad-looking cattle. Water was being trucked into some areas; house gardens that received dribbles from kitchen sinks were bedraggled; dust storms towered over landscapes. And politicians were turning up on the land with their Akubras and empty lamentations.

It's a form of torture to watch land die. The grass turns crisp and breakable. It scrunches and collapses beneath your feet. If you were barefoot, it would hurt. By the time grass is crispy, people stop using machinery because sparks will create a fire that might last the whole summer.

The ground goes hard. Concrete hard. It is baked in the kiln of summer. Just as people in cold parts of the earth can't dig graves during winter months, it would be hard to dig a grave in a summer of drought here. I tried to dig holes for a few small saplings and the spade bounced off the ground. It was like whittling concrete; the spade could only shift shards of soil. The soil was telling me to give up on revegetating for a while.

I was still watering the new plantings, but I would look across to the mature trees in the distance and wonder how they could survive months without a drink and years with just a dribble. Those trees dropped leaves and branches, their trunks became parched, but surprisingly few collapsed in the field. Some fell during windstorms but most stood sentinel, their trunks turned to husks, their branches jagged. You'd call them habitat trees in the city, but here they were just dead.

Animals were being hand-fed and the price of feed quadrupled. Trucks crisscrossed the continent, carrying a few days of nutrition for local herds. Appreciated but not enough. Dams receded to crazy-paving floors, creeks paused in puddles. It got hotter. A strange muteness enveloped the land. Birdsong disappeared. I couldn't figure out whether the birds had left or were too flat to sing, and I didn't want to betray my ignorance by asking. The calls of cows and sheep seemed to disappear or grow weak. The hum of machinery fell quiet.

People stopped talking on the street: a head nod instead and then move on. You give head nods at funerals. By then, talk of rain was not invited. I realised that drought was a silent squeeze. The media calls it the 'grip of drought', the 'vice-like grip' and that's the gist. It sits heavy over the land and is felt like a squeeze on shoulders, on hearts, even on the ability to talk.

One day in January, a busy time in the vineyard, we'd been training vines since 6 am and hoping to work until 1 pm when the temperature was due to reach 38 degrees. It got there before midday. I was racing to get work done. Not a good idea.

Then I noticed two vines that had been trained the wrong way, meaning I'd have to unhook them from the wire, cut deeply down their trunk and start them over. I lost it. 'What the fuck are we doing here?' I yelled to Roger. 'I mean, what the fuck?'

I was complaining about the wrong training, but really I was yelling at the drought, at the heat, at the stupidity of growing anything in a landscape where good years were the exception. At the silliness of two middle-aged and rapidly ageing people thinking they could grow wine; at our ineptitude; at our silly, city optimism. At fucking everything.

And we'd only been trying for a few years. Other farmers had been working the land for half a century. Other farmers had been working in this drought for seven or eight years; other farmers didn't have a city escape, a little job on the side; other farmers had all their capital and most of their family history tied to land that now looked like an empty car park. Other farmers were real farmers, not hobbyists from the city.

It would be easy to give up on the country in drought. Walk away. Buy a unit in the city and never look inland again. Once again I began wondering why country people hang around for all those Dorothea Mackellar horrors. Some do walk off the land, but most stay, hoping for another go, hoping they don't have to get a job with Bunnings in the city.

Even as I thought this, it occurred to me that Roger and I hadn't thought about walking away. Except for a few moments of hot temper, we were still doing the work required. Maybe it isn't that easy to walk away. Even in the three years we'd been working the land, we now felt invested. The compulsion to make good the labour and money we'd invested in the land was stuck.

Economists refer to this as the sunk-cost fallacy; others know it as throwing good money after bad. But there's a moment when throwing more resources at a problem won't solve the problem and not many can recognise that moment. And, keeping an economist's hat on, there is an opportunity cost to staying with it. We should, they say, look ahead and see what opportunities remain if we stay, and what opportunities we might miss if we stay. Economists look ahead; farmers look to history, to the toil that's been invested, to their thickened knuckles, buried livestock. To the swings slung over creeks for children and the dreams they have overlaid across this wide brown land. Such different perspectives. One might be more rational, but neither is right.

I stopped talking about the weather by midsummer. Nobody wanted to hear, and I didn't want to bear that news. By then, the air was thick not just with dust but with smoke. A horrendous fire season was bringing smoke from the Southern Highlands, from the outskirts of Canberra and from the Snowy Mountains. For winegrowers, the smoke was as big a threat as the fire. It doesn't take much smoke to ruin the taste of wine—half an hour of heavy smoke can do it—and this area was bathed in smoke for weeks.

While I checked the weather forecast each morning, other winegrowers walked out to check the smoke. We were lucky only in the sense that our grapes were too young to harvest; we just had to keep the vines alive.

I stopped looking at the weather forecast so often. I looked just once a day, noted the information and didn't give it weight. Do what you can do with what has been given you.

I tried to convince myself that, no matter what the forecast, I should proceed as if the drought would continue for a long time. But, in truth, I kept looking and couldn't help feeling hopeful at the promise of a 50 per cent chance of precipitation in a week. Sometimes, I would set my gaze on the horizon and try to will rain clouds to form. But hope is not a rainmaker. And, as that woman who spoke at the regeneration conference said, it's time to take hope out of farming.

13

Husband Gets a
Fridge Magnet

Roger wanted to replace the lock on one of our outside doors. He declares his intention out of the blue, but it's obvious that he's been thinking about it, researching it and planning it. And he has resolved to do it. I groan inwardly, and a bit outwardly.

Roger is not good at handy stuff. He knows it; he's been told it; he has history with it. Ever since he was young, his father Bill has told him that he is hopeless at doing stuff with his hands. His father, a mechanic, would ask Roger to help with a job or would try to instruct Roger in a job, and the result was always the same. Bill would decide the effort was hopeless; he would lash out at Roger, grab the tools back and tell his son that he was too hopeless to get a proper trade—such as a mechanic.

Throughout his youth, Roger heard the refrain: if he couldn't improve his skills, he would end up working for the council—and that usually meant working as a garbo. Growing up to be a garbo was obviously the go-to threat of parents in post-war Australia. I heard it, my brothers heard it and Roger heard it. It was the end of the line.

Roger wasn't too fussed about the garbo threat because, as a surfer, he knew that having the hours and wage of a garbo would enable him to surf all day. Besides, he knew he had other skills.

It has always amazed me that Roger's father never imagined a bigger future for his son. The most he envisaged was that Roger would follow in his footsteps with a trade and, if that failed, then it was down to the council depot for him. He never seemed to think that Roger could do better—better than his father.

Roger would do better. He would become a journalist and an editor, he would start up various publications and, at one stage, run Australia's financial daily. He would be more influential and more financially secure than his father, without ever mastering the correct way to hold a hammer. One day he might even become a winegrower.

We lived happily for many decades on the principle that if something was broken you found an expert to fix it. Sometimes we'd call the expert immediately; at other times we called the expert after Roger had tried to fix it. I tried not to echo his father when Roger decided to fix whatever had broken, but I did try to ring an expert before he got started on the job.

The farm changed this. I don't know if it was the influence of Ian and his competence at bloody everything, or whether Roger had intuited that people in the country are too proud to call for help on a job that everyone else in the country knows how to fix. Roger wanted to fix things himself.

When he declared his intention with the door lock, I did a quick inventory of what would be needed and what might go wrong. The new lock might not be the right size—that seemed very likely, given the dimensions and wonkiness of the door. The receiving plate might be in the wrong spot. The quality of the door—hollow core—might thwart a new lock. The door might end up with no lock but an unfillable hole that would necessitate the replacement of the door. We might have to board up the door for ages while we waited for a handyman to come and replace it—no doubt giving us eye rolls about the mess we'd made.

Sure, I had little faith, but it was a tricky job for someone trained in words, concepts and the management of big egos.

It had to be done because he and Ian had installed a gun safe for some new guns and, according to their licence, police would inspect the storage of the guns, making sure that the safe was bolted to the floor and the wall, and that the house was lockable.

We later discovered that police never check country houses. Perhaps they know no one in the country locks their doors, even if they have well-fitted locks. Why lock the door if there's nothing worth stealing except for the guns in the safe? And, as gun safes must be fastened to a wall and a floor, a robber would have to remove a corner of the house to get the guns. When I look around our little house and imagine what might interest a robber, I see a new kettle ($29), expensive shampoo ($59) and an etching of a cockatoo that might not be to the taste of a robber. The rest isn't worth lugging to a getaway car.

I couldn't deter Roger from the task ahead, so I acted as his sous-chef. As we gathered around the door with tools, the new fittings and instructions, I held my breath. At what point would the lock fail to fit? Or the door buckle under the strain? Or the lock fail to turn, or the receiving plate fail to receive? I wondered when Roger would start swearing, or throwing the lock across the room, or accusing me of distracting him. At what point would I declare, 'It's just not working, let's call an expert'?

It didn't happen. What happened was the lock worked. Roger installed it straight and solid; it fitted into the receiving plate. It didn't have a hole around it; it just worked. Roger wasn't hopeless with his hands.

Since then, Roger has started fixing lots of things. And I don't panic about it. I don't even try to talk him out of it. And he mostly *does* fix them. The blades of the mower, screens that fall off, machinery that gets stuck, technology that freezes, devices that go blank, nozzles that block, blades that dull. That door lock seemed to break the cycle of defeat; maybe it silenced the critic sitting beside him and the one in his childhood. Sure, he takes his time and does a lot of research before he starts the job, but he can now do stuff with his hands. Maybe all he needed sixty years ago was a bit more time, more confidence, more understanding.

I wonder what his father would think now. But I believe I know. His father was too tough on his son and would probably still be tough. I suspect his father knew that Roger had a bigger future in front of him—one that was denied to his father. Maybe his father was trying to impress on his son that the skills of a mechanic were important, worthy of respect. Roger never felt disrespect for his father, but his father did to his son.

I can't change the past, but I can change the critic that still hovers around him today. *Shut up, Deirdre, and let him do the job. When he does the job, tell him that it's a good job. When he fixes something for you, say thank you.*

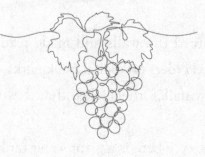

14

Pitter Patter

It's amazing what people can get used to. Whole populations can get used to living in a war zone; they can get on with their lives when a dictator takes away their dreams of the future; they can live through plagues and pestilence and still hang out the washing in the morning and cook dinner at night.

So, the country learned to live with drought. Farmers sold more livestock, bought more feed from the trucks criss-crossing the continent, extended mortgages and tried to change the subject when they chatted with neighbours in the supermarket. If there was hope, the expression of hope was in the jobs they were doing. Those whose dams had dried to crazy-paving patterns got tractors and dug them deeper, reinforced the walls and made ready for rainfall. Some kept seed orders on digital bookmarks, ready to click at the first downfall. Others joked that they never liked to bathe anyway.

We were lucky. There is a giant water tank on the property and two irregular users of it, so we could offer the family showers. 'Come and have a really long shower at our place,' we'd said to Mum and the sisters. 'Use the toilet and flush it straight away.' We were rich in household water and sometimes we diverted it to soak the vineyard, where the shallow-rooted vines hung on. We checked the vines often, watching for wilting leaves and digging up clods of earth beneath the grow lines to make sure there was some moisture in the soil. All the plants—vines, new trees, roses—were on life support. The country was in ICU. Life went on, even if it was a subdued, almost silent, life.

Then it changed.

One day in late summer, the locals almost at once began talking about a rain event expected the following week. Ian mentioned it when he was leaving. Mary said she'd heard chatter about it. Patrick was certain—'It's coming,' he said.

I don't know where their information came from, but suddenly activity picked up. There was a sense of urgency as everyone started planning around a rain event—buying seed, preparing machinery, booking contractors, finishing the digging of dams and, finally, permitting themselves to talk about it. Their knowledge, and their confidence in that knowledge, was so sudden; it was like they'd sniffed rain on the breeze or felt a rising under their feet. Maybe they just had a better weather app. And, of course, Mum's spring showed signs of life—a dribble at first, and then, within days, it started to flow.

The first rain arrived after almost four months of complete dry and three years of mostly dry. It was a half-decent fall, between 40 and 70 millimetres, but it was enough to give a moment of hope, to dampen the dust, to prove to everyone that rain could still happen. Over the next month two similar falls came. It wasn't a flood, it wasn't enough to break the formal drought, but it was enough. It was enough to grow pasture while the weather remained warm. It was enough to dribble into dams; it was enough to feed the roots of mature trees and allow regular summer growth from the gum saplings.

A few more falls arrived and the hand-feeding of livestock stopped, the supply of livestock to sales yards slowed. The ground grew soft and friable, the spade dug deep into clods of soil and the old roses bloomed with a late flowering. Creeks were flushed out, stores in town ordered more supplies and the pace of everything picked up, busy and louder. A breath was released, from people and the land.

I still checked the forecasts, but without the dread of the previous months. It was more from curiosity and, perhaps, greed for more. I stopped talking about it again, partly because it wasn't necessary but also because it still felt too soon. You don't talk about the weather when the memory of its torture is still fresh—beating you into the ground, tearing at your heart. And causing you to drop your gaze so you don't have to see the horizon, or to see the trees turned to husks and the eyes of neighbours passing in the street.

The drought ended not with a sigh but with a rush.

15

You Don't Know Me, but You Know My Mum

If someone were to ask me the most important thing to have in the country, I'd have a list. Reliable rainfall, not too many weeds, a haphazard attitude to nail care, a big hat, a boot scraper, gloves that fit properly and good relationships. And the last one is the most important.

It's easy to underestimate the value of community relationships when you first arrive from the city where we too easily treat people as resources to be traded, wrangled and made expendable on the basis that other resources are around the corner. Not in the country.

Mum has always known the importance of relationships and, indeed, she is known around town as a good citizen. That means she hires local, pays people on time and treats everyone with respect, and if she's not treated with respect she quietly lets that relationship slip.

Slowly, and sometimes painfully, I've picked up tips for relating in the countryside and, in no particular order, here's a list of them.

Hire local, but don't let them think they're permanent. Everyone knows that a country town will only survive if everyone supports each other. So you look for local tradespeople; if you don't you'll pay for it eventually. For instance, a local builder told me that some people will hire building teams out of Canberra, even though those builders charge more. But when those houses need repairs, they'll contact him. 'Give me the crumbs,' as he put it. He'll do the work, but he'll do it on his timetable and he'll charge Canberra prices for the job.

Buy local. And if you don't, people will notice. For instance, it's an unspoken rule that if you buy a ute you buy a Toyota from the town dealer. You don't have to, but if your European ute breaks down you'll wait a while for a mechanic and the mechanic will charge the sort of prices that the Sydney European car–servicing centres charge.

Ditto, if you buy a device that needs installing. If you walk out the door without making an appointment for installation, the retailer may give you the impression that you've stolen something from them. And what's worse is that when you ask other people to install it, they'll wonder why you're asking them and not using the original retailer. The presumptions they'll make won't reflect well on you.

If you're from the city, service people will treat you differently. And not just because you use the expression 'service people'. Whenever we had to get a job done, I quickly learned to open the conversation with, 'Hi, my name is Deirdre and I'm Ann's daughter.' When I did that, they would almost always say something like 'Oh yeah, what would you like?' or 'How is the little lady?' If I didn't declare my link with a local, they would politely take my details, get the gist of the job and say they'd get back to me when they could. And sometimes they would get back to me. Sometimes not.

This can make newcomers feel unwelcome, but it's more to do with loyalty. You prioritise people who have been your customers for years—or decades—and only take a punt on new customers when your old mates have been served. Mum has built up three decades of social capital in town and we're trading on it a lot.

Women aren't always welcome in shops. Okay, I mean hardware and farming suppliers. I have stood in front of a counter with three men behind the counter—one serving the only other customer, while the two idle men look straight past me. There was none of this 'Can I help you?' Or 'What can I do for you, love?' Or even a 'Next!' Their gaze simply didn't include me in it, even though I was right in front of them.

Momentarily, I wondered if I had jumped a queue. I glanced behind and saw no one. There was no queue.

So, I asked for service: 'Can I pick up the package that was ordered a few hours ago?' I asked. The old guy looked taken aback for a moment, like he'd just spotted a ghost and then pushed towards me the package that was sitting on the counter.

This attitude isn't just for city women. My mother—big sheep farmer, wool classer, emeritus professor, reliable paymaster and resident of thirty years' standing—still feels the sting of the 'wise old men', as she describes them. Those wise old men tell her what she should be doing, what she's doing wrong, what they intend to do for her, when they're going to do it and how they're going to do it their way. She's polite to them, but she holds the chequebook, so they will usually do it her way. If not, they become someone she used to know.

Timetables work differently. It is strange that, no matter what service you want in the country, you have to fit in with the service provider's timetable. For example, when we contacted an irrigation plumber to fix pipes he'd installed a few months previously, he took us through his timetable, reciting where and when he was going to be working over the next few weeks and then declared he wouldn't be in our area for another two weeks. His base was only 12 kilometres away, which is virtually next door in the country.

Or, another time, he told us he should have a free hour some time in next few weeks, so he'd let us know when he was arriving at our address (that sort of arrangement isn't much good when we're likely to be 300 kilometres away in Sydney when he happens by).

Sometimes, when the job is big, like moving a flock of sheep onto a truck, you will line up all the farm workers who will be needed, plus the boss woman, and wait for the appointed truck. And then be told he's going to be a few hours late, because he's picked up another job down the highway.

This brings us to the core challenge of working with others in the country—you haven't got a big choice. There may be three plumbers in town, but one is always too far away, one is not well regarded, and the other one knows he's the only decent plumber in town and can pick his clients. The first challenge is to find someone who can tell you who is the right plumber; when you get that name, you plead with said plumber to visit your property and you make sure the tea and cake are ready when he arrives. Then, after a few times of working with them, you will find yourself in a magic circle of can-do people.

When you find your plumber/electrician/viticulturalist, they will connect you with people in their network. For instance, if we hadn't met Richard, the viticulturalist, we wouldn't have met Chrissie and Brooke or our winemaker, Alex. If we hadn't grabbed Ian's number from an advertisement pinned to the wall of the local pub, we might not have a vineyard.

Everyone is related to, or at least known to, others, so don't say mean things about others. Chatting to a local one day, I mentioned that the owner of a business in town was trying to sell a building that was full of asbestos, so it would be a bugger to renovate. She replied, 'Oh yes, my father-in-law doesn't know what to do with that place.' *Ahhhhhh.*

Some people, like Ian, seem to know everyone—living and dead. He is partly related to half the people we mention; he has worked with most of them and won't do work again for a few of them. People like Ian are like those digital rating systems that are used in online commerce. You don't want to get a one-star rating in the country.

It's easy to get the feeling there is a giant web that stretches across the land, connecting everyone and tripping up newcomers. There are circles in which you will be a preferred client, but you won't know they exist until you either get into that circle or find that nobody is returning your calls. Without referrals, your life is over.

Status is determined not by money or education or even manners, but by how long you've lived in the area and the size of your footprint on the land. Some people in town have landmarks named after them or, rather, their ancestors. It might be a street, a creek, a building, a park or civic centre. These landmark families are descendants of original settlers, who showed up shortly after Hume laid marks for the highway connecting Sydney and Melbourne.

Some landmark families are wealthy, but many have wayward members of the family, who take consolation from sharing the name of a creek or a street. The squattocracy still holds sway in country circles, even if city folk view their heritage with suspicion, given the way the country was claimed for settlement.

Under the protocols of settlement, the newest people in town occupy the bottom rung of society, even if they are bankers with a penchant for winemaking. Perhaps especially then. A newcomer might win favour by providing an essential service, such as coffee or a restaurant; they might get a nod in the street if they have bought an expensive tractor. But they are outsiders for a long, long time.

Then there's the footprint. Many properties in the area are hobby farms, roughly 25 acres (10 hectares—most still talk in acres) which is big enough for a horse or two and a kitchen garden. They're not farmers. They're called hobby farmers or tree-changers or lifestyle farmers, but they're not called farmers. To be treated like a farmer takes a couple of hundred acres.

If you have enough land to run several hundred sheep or a few score of cattle, then the locals will acknowledge that you're farming. A cute farm. If you have a few thousand acres, then you're taken much more seriously. Chances are your farm is known to many locals; they may even have known the previous owners or have read about the original claimants. These farms usually have a name on the front gate and a homestead, whose floors and walls were constructed from timbers and stones found on the property. But if you have, say, 25,000 acres, well—Hello, Rupert Murdoch!

Ovine royalty still reigns here. But sometimes it's hard to spot. There are grand houses from the nineteenth century; houses bearing plaques from visiting royals; houses with servants' quarters, ballrooms, a manager's cottage and heritage gardens. There are broad-acre sheep stations— like Cavan, the one owned by the Murdoch family—that occupy most of the horizon when you drive past. There are families who walk the same hallways as their great-great-grandparents and some have sheep that can trace a similar lineage. Strangely, it's hard to find a list of these properties. Perhaps they like it that way.

Locals don't like it when established broadacre farms are carved up into lifestyle parcels. I'm not sure why, but perhaps it's the loss of heritage, the loss of another serious farm or maybe they don't like the people that lifestyle farms attract (they're not going to like me after this little analysis). But I suspect it's the diversity of farm sizes and the diversity of activity on those farms that have kept the Yass Valley vibrant. From the half-acre homes in town, to the hobby lots on the edge of town and the medium-sized farms in the Valley, right out to the heritage spreads around the Murrumbidgee River, the area has retained a family community and a farming culture.

Other towns in the state have faded as their population dropped below the critical level for maintaining services. Many of the big country towns have lost too many residents; they've lost wealth because of previous busts and droughts; they've bred a few too many wayward relatives and they've lost their promising youth to the city. Their glory days were in another century.

Other areas have lost their farming communities to aggregation and commercial interests. The push to get big or get out has re-arranged the boundary fences across the country. Economic tides and demographic waves have reshaped most of Australia's rural areas and left some places bigger and others smaller.

What makes the difference? Being on a major road helps, as does being close to a capital city. A secure water supply— well, reasonably secure. The right sort of commodities at the right time. The right people all the time—having an energetic community and the luck of good leaders make a big difference. If there are enough people who believe in the future of their town, the town will have a future. There will be pony clubs and football teams and markets on Saturday and a local paper and fundraisers for families that meet with disaster.

The tipping point for a town's viability is hard to pick but, once reached, the trajectory becomes self-sustaining— whether it is growing or fading. And while it's quaint to have a town where some people can trace their dining room buffet to a nineteenth-century relative, towns need more than that.

Towns need to replenish their people; they need an inflow of people to grow, regenerate, bring new ideas and ensure the town merits a Woolies and a Toyota dealer. They need dreamers, even if those newcomers don't know a flower from a weed, or a tractor from a digger, or a lamb from a hogget. Maybe, they need new residents so the established residents can get over themselves. (And I may have just broken another rule of the country.)

1 6

Locals Only

Covid arrives. In the world, in Australia, in Sydney and, as of two weeks ago, it arrives in town. We didn't bring it to town, but some stares from locals suggest it may as well have been us. The virus spreads, the world closes down and country towns close themselves off to outsiders in scores of subtle and not-so-subtle ways.

We're outsiders. Sort of. The police cars tucked away in culverts along the highway would regard us as outsiders. We prepare to answer their questions as we drive down the mostly deserted highway on the Easter weekend.

Where are you going?

To work.

Really?

Yes. Just look at my fingernails.

Then they might look inside our car and note the food baskets, boxes of wine and, if we're lucky, the air compressor.

Look officer, we have farming equipment in the back. We're not going on a picnic.

It's not a wrong answer, but it might not be the answer they accept.

The reason we're carrying a lot of food and stores with us is that we've been told that signs in the town supermarket warn we'll be asked to show identification and, if the address isn't local, we're not welcome. I get it. Shelf raiders from Canberra have made locals chary. They want their air to be virus-free and their shelves full of toilet paper.

We've also been told that the police in town will question us if we drive down the main street. How will they know if our car is local or FOREIGN? Are our hubcaps too clean? Should we have a kelpie in the back?

Radio broadcasts repeat that non-essential travel is banned. Double negative. Lots of negatives. We're essential, I say to myself in preparation for a grilling. We're essential to the vines downed by an autumn blast; to the eradication of weeds spreading after rains; to the winter pruning that will determine next year's harvest. It will be our first harvest, but just saying that sounds presumptuous. Nothing seems certain now.

I read somewhere that wine is an essential industry. Should have taken a screen shot of that. *Look officer, do you want a glass of wine with your dinner when you finish your shift or not?* Besides, the vineyard house is hardly a weekender. I should carry on me photos of the basic set-up: the bare and buckling kitchen, the 1970s carpet, the mix-n-match furniture and, most tellingly, the lack of wi-fi and TV. Look officer, can you see a weekender in this photo? Is this where you would go for leisure?

I get why they do it. Second homes seem too bourgeois to be tolerated in a pandemic. For those who have the luxury of an escape house, it's difficult to convince authorities that they need to be there. Officer, I need to restock the wine fridge, dead-head the roses and let Brutus have a run in the meadow.

But it still hurts those who feel a belonging to both, and perhaps a bigger fondness for the getaway. Asked to nominate which place feels more like home, Roger would now say the vineyard. Not I. Sydney remains home, but I'd miss the Hill if I couldn't get there.

As we roll out of the city, onwards to the vineyard, the highway unspools before us. It feels like we have escaped from a city that has become a petri dish. It has too many residents, too many surfaces, too many mouths breathing, too many lungs exhaling.

I imagine a Bruegel painting and realise that this pandemic feels almost medieval. It reeks of those bygone times of plagues, when citizens collapsed in ditches, an army of skeletons marched across the blackened land and wayfarers were the bogeymen of the highways. Gypsies. Minstrels. Saracens. Tinkers. Freemen. Mercenaries. Those who took to the roads were treated with suspicion; travellers were treated as carriers and always, when plagues arrived, others were blamed.

The Other, ever the handy target. During the Black Death of the fourteenth century, some thought the plague was caused by Jews poisoning wells. The Great Plague of London in 1665 was blamed on Jesuits, those Catholic priests who travelled to distant places. Cholera outbreaks in New York in the nineteenth century were blamed on newly arrived Irish Catholics. Chinese immigrants got shafted for smallpox outbreaks in San Francisco in the late nineteenth century. Epidemics make exiles of people in their own country, as Albert Camus wrote in *The Plague*.

Yet it was the travelling salesmen who opened up trade between fourteenth-century towns; it was trade that created a global economy in the nineteenth century; it was globalisation that knitted Chinese factory workers, Australian farmers, Indian pharmacists and Silicon Valley engineers into a common market. And, yeah, it's globalisation that has brought plague from a food market in China to our town of 6000 people in southern New South Wales.

The world just got smaller and if you don't live in town then you're the outsider. Or, as a friend said to me as we prepared to depart for the vineyard, 'You're an absent land-lord. That's as bad as carrying the plague.' We are more like absent tenants, given our name is not on the deeds, but no one likes a chancer.

As the highway, spookily sparse of traffic, peels down to two lanes, I wonder whether the place down the road feels home enough to call home. What makes it home? It's certainly not the title deed, absent of our names. It might be whether you check your mailbox, but that seems too slight a claim. It could be based on how many jars of spices are in the pantry or how many plants you can name in its garden. It's partly how much time you spend there, but I think it's more to do with how much you labour there.

Have you planted a garden, tended a garden and watched as sheep manure becomes flowers? Have you cleared junk? *Oh yes.* Have your repaired buildings? *Tick!* Have you planted a future in the field? *Yes, 2300 times, now that the second vineyard is in place.* Have you kept an eye on the animals that grow fat there, or the birds that visit the trees and sometimes pillage the crops?

Do you know where the sun rises, where the frost settles and the names of the first birds to sing in the morning? *Tick!* Do you know who to call for a plumbing problem, an escaped animal, roofing, electricals, clapped-out machinery? *Hello, Ian.* More to the point: will they answer your call? Does the barmaid know your name?

I don't think the highway officer would ask us those questions. He might just look at our clothes. Or our wine selection. Or clock how clean the wheel rims are.

We arrive at last, unhitching the gate, unloading supplies and taking a breath of chilled autumn air. Sure, we're here to work, but we are here for safety too. The ability to move about without washing our hands every few seconds and without dodging those five million Sydneysiders who are trying to exercise in a city where most places for doing so have been closed. We are here to unwrap our own food, clean our own bathrooms and switch off the radio news to listen to the sounds of nature.

Home is where you feel safest. Where all the pathogens are your own. And, okay, home is also where the first mouse of the winter is seeking warmth inside. Does setting a mouse trap make it home?

Maybe I could tell the highway police that this home is where I feel a sense of belonging, a place where my spirit feels settled. But even as I have this thought, I realise that it doesn't hold weight in a country where the original inhabitants have never been granted the same recognition.

The weight of Aboriginal peoples' dispossession—which may only be felt by white inhabitants as a theoretical pain, as an injustice, as a reason to protest—feels heavier now. Who are they—those in uniforms and parliaments—to tell us where we call home? How can they dismiss what we feel about place, whatever feeling that is, so lightly?

Maybe links to the land for all Australians are fragile. The original inhabitants didn't rely on legal papers to prove their connection, the settlers didn't bother too much with them either (squattocracy, anyone?) and the generations since have—knowingly or not—felt the tenuousness of their foothold on the land. Today, even if you have a legal document, they can declare it void for the duration of an emergency.

So our sense of belonging to the funny-shaped Hill isn't shared and isn't recognised. It's the vibe; it's our vibe, but try explaining that vibe to a police officer leaning in the driver's window. It's a belonging tolerated in good times but made redundant in bad times. And these are bad times.

Eventually, Roger and I will be forced to choose. Not for the pandemic. Not even for tax purposes or for the highway cops. But maybe because one of us feels the pull to belong to the second home, to put the second home first.

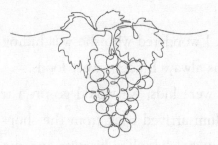

17

A Bake-off

I had baked a cake for Mum's visit. It was an apple crumble cake and, if split three ways, it was big enough for an afternoon tea for Roger and me, a few nights of dessert for my sister Mary and her husband Stefan, and a week of eating for Mum and Ray.

Sometimes I think about giving Mum less cake—not because she's undeserving, but because I'm worried she will keep it until it turns into Miss Havisham's wedding cake. Once I suggested she store the cake I was handing to her in the fridge, but she said she had a special place for it and pulled a container from a bottom drawer. She then tucked the cake away down there under some trays where nobody would find it. I wondered who she was hiding it from, but then Mum has always hidden sweet foods.

When we were kids, we would go on a treasure hunt every time Mum arrived back from the shops because we knew she'd bought chocolate biscuits and she would have hidden them—somewhere. So we'd start at the pantry—up high behind the old tins, or down low among the potatoes. Then we'd move to the platter cupboards and rummage behind them, and then to the formal dining room and open the silverware drawers. Sometimes we would have to look under the banquette seats in the entrance before we found the biscuits. But we always found them. Mum hasn't changed the habit; now I'm wondering if she's hiding them from herself.

I'm not sure when I became a baker for my country family. I don't remember making any decision. I suspect I just took them some leftover cake one day and was flabbergasted by how appreciative everyone was. So, I did it again. Then I did it every visit. Now if I occasionally arrive without a cake I can see Stefan looking perplexed—like a labrador that has been promised a treat and starts licking empty hands.

Cake was once currency in the country. You wouldn't dream of turning up without a batch of scones, slices or a freshly creamed cake. And for good reason. Distances were great, trips to the shop rare, friendly visits almost as rare. Cakes gave cachet. They said you were a considerate visitor, a capable baker and, in the early days, a poultry farmer, butter churner and a housewife who knew how to keep weevils out of flour.

Today the trip into town is ten minutes, there are half-a-dozen shops selling cakes and no one will go hungry if you arrive without a cake tin. But there is something about a homemade cake, and most of it is that it shows you were thinking of them even when they were far away. It is love folded with a spatula.

But some of its appeal is the idea that a homemade cake isn't as bad for you as a shop-bought one. That it has better fats, fewer calories; that you are somehow immune to the fat-forming outcome of cake because it is homemade.

It's not true. I know exactly how much butter and sugar goes into those babies

While sharing the apple crumble cake with Mum, I mentioned that I wanted to replace the lounge room's green carpet. It was half-a-century old, had faded into a snot-coloured pile and would probably collapse into a million bits of fibre if

I attempted to steam-clean it. She may have felt cornered because, as we shared the slice, a tradeswoman from the local carpet shop arrived to measure up the lounge room.

'The carpet seems fine,' Mum said.

'Well, it has lots of damage under the lounges, there is water damage near the door and red wine stains that are impossible to spot-clean,' I replied. 'Besides, I'll pay for it.' (Negotiating repairs to the house is, well, a negotiation. As it is owned by Mum and Ray, we usually operate on a landlord/tenant basis. They finance repairs to the house and we pay for décor items.)

She took another bite of the cake as the tradie asked if we wanted a quote for the removal of the old carpet. I said yes.

'We could use the old carpet for the bedrooms of the hunting lodge,' Mum suggested, referring to the shed–house on a property she had recently bought. 'It would make the bedrooms feel more loved,' she added.

Mum doesn't like to throw things out. In fact, I think she's incapable of it. To her, everything deserves another go unless it is toxic, turning to dust in her hands or growing mould on its icing—in which case, she'll just cut the mouldy bit off.

We used to think her thrift was due to her early years in the Great Depression, even though her family was unscathed by its hardships. Then we thought it was because she had to raise ten kids on Dad's union wage, even though he soon began earning a barrister's wage. Sometimes we attributed it to her desire to keep her children slim, even though we managed to bulk up, helped along by hidden biscuit stashes. More recently, we think it's because she is environmentally minded—and she encourages this explanation.

Really, her thrift is all of those things, but it's also something else. Mum likes the challenge of making resources stretch. She is a born economist (and an educated economist) and sees the world as resources that can be used well or used inefficiently. She would add that they are God-given resources (she's also religious) and it is our duty to use what God has given as well as we can.

Surely God didn't mean for a snot-coloured carpet to last more than half a century. But I didn't say that to her. When I want to convince Mum, I have to use my economic brain:

'Mum, I don't think the lounge room carpet will make the journey in one piece over to the hunting lodge. But the bedroom carpets are in better nick so, when I replace them, I'll get the old carpets over there.'

Mum nodded but didn't say anything. She had a mouthful of cake. I took it as a sign of agreement, albeit a reluctant agreement, and before we could continue the debate I scribbled a signature on the carpet order and bustled the tradeswoman out to her car.

Mum is not mean with money. She does, for instance, spend money on tractors. She's just upgraded buggies to safer versions; she spends money on fences and safer holding pens for sheep. She invests in watering systems, in solar energy; she restocks the livestock rapidly and plants pastures for feed.

But all of this is investment: it's investing in the productive capacity of the land. Carpet isn't productive. Even if the sight of snot-green carpet makes one of her volunteer labourers feel like fleeing back to the city.

Mostly, Mum buys properties. If you want to grab her attention, all you have to say is, 'I think there's a property for sale around the corner.' Indeed, that's the way she came to own most of her properties. I think she owns nine farms now. And about four or five town properties. I'm not sure what the tally is, but they would be worth many millions.

When you mention money of that size, it often points to greed. But I don't think Mum is greedy. She doesn't have fancy cars, expensive jewellery, wardrobes of designer gear or soaps from five-star hotels around the world, although, it must be said, her own carpet is only fifteen years old.

For her, acquiring another property is an opportunity for a creative project. She loves taking something that has been under-utilised and making it better—more productive, but often more environmentally sound too. In her own way, she's re-creating the land in line with her principles and, perhaps, in God's image.

I guess that's why she's rich and I'm her unpaid, but much-loved, labourer who was stuck with snot-green carpet for too long. But not much longer.

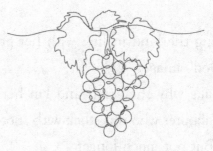

1 8

Boring My Kid,
Blooding the Next Gen

Toby is visiting for a few days. It is our son's first visit in almost three years; in fact he hasn't been here since we planted the first vineyard. Maybe we shouldn't have worked him so hard over that first week in November 2017. Still, he's obviously forgiven us.

It helps that he has been isolated in a Kings Cross flat for almost three months; he hasn't seen a stretch of green longer than the synthetic turf in his enclosed verandah since summer, he's been forced to take a week off work and he doesn't have a girlfriend. (As I write this, I realise we are way down his list of priorities.)

He takes a deep breath on arrival and gazes out over the vines. He contemplates the countryside and is quiet. I'm reminded of a passage I've recently read in a biography of Hamilton Hume: 'Were it not for the explorers extending the boundaries of settlement, the community (in Sydney Cove) would have imploded in mutual loathing and rage. The explorers gifted it with a safety valve; the land itself, the immensity of its presence, the promise of its bounty.'

I feel like I've just done a motherly duty by providing my son with something that is vital for life. I must remind him of the benefits of getting into the country more often. In fact, over the next day and a half I do that constantly without mentioning it and without meaning to do it.

We show him the vineyard, point to the vines he planted and exclaim about how they've grown. We describe how we're going to spur-prune them in a few weeks, when he might visit again to help. We plant out a windbreak of bottlebrush on the southern end of riesling vineyard and I explain why a wind break is needed (rather pointlessly, given the wind vane is spinning like a roulette wheel). I point out how soft and friable the soil is after rain, why we put stones around the planting to protect it from weeds and rabbits and capture some warmth from the winter sun (God, I'm boring).

Roger and Toby try out the two new rifles. They hang balloons on a fence and blast them to bits. They're huntin' party balloons. (I don't say that, they're having too much fun.) Toby is a good shot; he might even be able to bag the fox that inhabits the western side of the Hill—a fox that is no doubt looking forward to the birth of about 600 lambs in the next few months.

Toby notices that a few sheep are bleating constantly and worrying a fence line that keeps them from the main flock. He sees a muster form; soon there is the car, the buggy and some encouraging yells at the half-dozen isolated sheep, plus strategic manoeuvring around two gates. For the next ten minutes, as I make tea in the kitchen, the Hill echoes with the sound of Toby and Roger's shouts, revving engines and the excited bleats. And then the sound of the buggy hurtling back up the Hill tells me they've done it.

Toby beams. Hunter: *tick!* Grazier: *tick!*

We light the fire pit and sit around it with beers as the sun begins to dip behind the Hill, and I wonder why we don't light the fire more often. To reheat some home-made moussaka, we set up the new Weber barbecue that we brought down and I point out that if Toby were down here with friends he could either use the fire pit as a barbecue or the Weber. *Boring, Deirdre.*

We have my sisters over for dinner and eat my tarte tatin (it was so-so). We visit Toby's grandmother and I suddenly feel guilty that he hasn't seen her for so long, but I wonder if they have missed each other. To miss someone, you have to spend time with each other.

These two—so similar in many ways—haven't seen each other much, firstly because Mum was always so busy but now because Toby is so busy. What's that Harry Chapin song? 'Cat's in the Cradle'. Even today, Toby's first memory of visiting his grandmother in the country is of all the sheep poo that stuck to his shoes.

Toby also visits two of his cousins, who have just become parents. I wonder how he feels, looking at his younger cousins nursing newborn babies. Distant, I guess. Old, probably. Or, more likely, urban. We introduce Toby to Ian, the agriculture magician, and to Patrick, who is father of the baby Toby just met. And we explain exactly how Ian is refiguring the shearing shed and the holding pens outside it to enable endless varieties of herding (yep, I'm really boring).

Toby and I take the buggy halfway up the Hill to a fold in the north-east face of the Hill. This is where Ian has suggested a shed could be built.

The question of where on the property to build a shed has been occupying Roger and me and Ian and Mum for weeks. It's been a frustrating exercise because on 100 hectares there are so many options, and yet none is an obvious choice.

Having debated for a while the six most obvious locations, it dawned on me that we were splitting along aesthetic lines and gender lines. Mum and I mostly agreed; Roger and Ian mostly agreed. The blokes favoured sites that were a rational choice for the uses that the shed would provide—but these made the shed prominent on the landscape. Mum and I wanted to scale down the visual impact of the shed and wouldn't have it near majestic trees or anywhere where it could disrupt the line of the Hill.

When you gaze at the Hill from our home compound, its conical shape against the sky makes the farm look like it's wearing a hat. Sometimes I felt silly explaining to Ian why the aesthetics of a shed wouldn't work in a particular spot especially if it spoiled the outline of the hatted Hill. I could almost see an eye roll. But I didn't care. It was important to me. And to Mum. And Mum pays the bills, so whatever she says is the final word.

One morning, a few weeks ago, Ian arrived and charged up to our house in his ute. 'I wonder what idea he has now,' Roger had said. He'd seen Ian arrive like this before. Sure enough, Ian had new ideas, including that of building the shed halfway up the Hill in the north-east fold.

So here are Toby and I now halfway up the Hill, checking out the view. The view is lovely and, somehow, the idea of a shed morphs into an plan for a cabin and it occurs to me that Toby and I see the land through city eyes (that is, envisaging a cute cabin for farm stays) whereas Ian and

Roger are seeing through country eyes (a place to house the ugly tractor). Toby goes higher than me, and at every step he takes I complain that he's just added another $10,000 to the cost of a gravel driveway (it's already looking like a half-kilometre of drive).

With the green fields and half-full dams, the vista from north to south is awesome; even to the west, behind us, the Hill is dotted with alpine mossy rocks that resemble a traditional painting by a First Nations artist. Every angle of this view is stunning. We shift up and down the Hill and move sideways, all within a 20-square-metre area, finding the perfect spot for catching winter sun, sheltering from south-westerly winds and avoiding summer afternoon sun. We settle around a group of rocks. 'Maybe,' I say to Toby, 'one day you could build a house up here and I could rebuild the house in the compound.'

As soon as I say it, I realise this is what these two days have been about. We want Toby to love this land as much as we do. We've been conducting a show-and-tell for two days. This has been our pitch, our 'deck' as Toby might say. It's not that we want him to move here right now, to buy an Akubra and graduate from shootin' balloons to huntin' foxes, but we want him to mark it as a possibility somewhere in his future. We want to show him why we love it. We want

1 9

Recollections of Rubbish

I have a problem with rubbish. Maybe, I should say, 'My name is Deirdre and I am a neat-aholic.' This mea culpa comes as I sit on the couch, gazing blankly at the wood burner and the scattering of burning embers on the hearth tiles that could have torched the house, ignited my socked feet or, at least, burnt a hole in the new carpet. All because of a slip of a receipt. A supermarket receipt.

Let me explain. I'd spotted the receipt lying on the kitchen bench and did what I always do with bits of paper, packaging, newspaper and anything else that once was a tree. I picked it up, opened the wood burner and tossed it into the flames. I hadn't noticed that a log was leaning against the inside of the heater door when I opened it, but

I did notice, just in time, as the log began to fall out. So I slammed the door closed and caught the log between the door and the burner. A save, sort of.

The log was still burning and now emitting smoke into the lounge room. It hadn't fallen out onto the tiles and possibly onto my socked feet, so I was grateful for that. However, it was still wedged in the door, burning away, and I could neither shut the door nor let the door go.

Some situations are so stupid, it takes a while to figure what just happened. I took stock. I was safe, because the door handle doesn't get hot and the log was far enough away from the handle to spare me its heat. The log shouldn't be allowed to fall out because it could roll anywhere—preferably onto tiles, but possibly onto carpet or feet. So my job was to manoeuvre the log back into the burner.

Roger was in the field, I was alone in the house and my phone was on the charger in the bedroom. I looked over to the poker stand and realised it was too far away for me to reach it without letting go of the door handle. I looked at the log again, trying to gauge how long it would take to burn down to nothing and whether I could hold the door against it until it was ash. By then, my hand was getting hot.

Stupid, stupid, stupid. But I couldn't spend time berating myself, and I couldn't let myself sniffle a few tears or start yelling for Roger. After a few more minutes of cursing myself, I noticed an unburnt log within reach. Hah.

I grabbed that log, pressed it against the bottom of the burning log, eased the door open a smidge and shoved the red-hot log into the burner. With a quick shove, pivot and slam of the door, I had the log back in the burner and only a few extra embers scattered across the tiles.

As I said, I have a problem. The business of rubbish has become an obsession. If I'm kind to myself, I might say I have gamified the business of rubbish. But when faced with the stupidity of nearly burning down the house for the sake of disposing of a supermarket receipt, I admit to obsession and wonder whether it's serious enough to get a doctor's referral to a specialist with a soft voice, non-judgemental manner and a comfy couch.

So let me lie on the proverbial couch for a moment and see if I can rationally explain my rubbish focus.

After spending a good year or so cleaning up the property from decades of neglect, I have zero tolerance for stuff left lying around the place. If Roger or Patrick or Ian or any visiting tradie leaves something on the ground, I notice it immediately. For the sake of peace, I might ignore it for a few days to give them a chance to sort it, and then I'm onto it. It's out. It's stowed or it's onto the back of their ute for them to sort. Maybe I have a touch of PTSD, but there's no way this property is going to slip back into a state of decay.

There are many studies showing that litter attracts more litter; that junk sets a standard for more junk. And if something is left around long enough to kill the grass beneath it then it's become the de facto storage spot for stuff. But not on my watch.

The other rationale for behaving like a madwoman with a Nifty Nabber, as the local hardware store tags them (and yes I have thought about buying one), is that living in the country forces you to confront your waste on a regular, and often visceral, basis. In short, whatever you bring into your house will have to be disposed of. By you. Sometimes with gloved hands and a held breath.

On the land, there are no garbage trucks that drive past your home with giant blades to lift your wheelie bins. Therefore, there's no reason to have wheelie bins—there's nowhere to wheel them. We don't even have a bin; just two small tidy-bins in the kitchen for waste and recyclables. Rubbish is managed manually from the moment you bring it onto your property—no matter how smelly, drippy or toxic it becomes.

So, I've developed a system. Firstly, you have to be careful what you bring into the house. Roger, for instance, can only buy beer in cans because bottles are too heavy and cumbersome to cart out.

If we buy something with a lot of packaging, we remove the packaging at the store, or just outside, and leave it (responsibly) for the store to sort out. They might get the message if enough people do this.

We use recyclable bags to carry groceries, try to buy loose produce and, if a plastic bag is needed for the fruit and vegetables, we find ways to re-use it in the kitchen or tool room. We buy only what we need to eat for the next day or two and avoid bulk-buy specials, because they inevitably don't get used in time. We are nifty shoppers, not because we're frugal, and not even because we're green, but because we don't want to spend time as garbos.

By the time stuff becomes waste, there is another system in place. As I mentioned, anything that used to be a tree goes into the wood burner; if it's too big for that, it goes onto the fire pit, where it works as kindling, and, if it's really big, like broken timber furniture, it goes out to the field pile to await a winter burn-off. And, by the by, the charcoal from those fires eventually gets distributed over the rose beds, which benefit from the added carbon, although I'm not sure they appreciate ash from supermarket receipts.

135

Food waste is a bit of a problem. I should have a compost heap but I'm afraid of creating a cosy home for snakes close to the house. So I have started throwing old fruit and vegetables out onto the paddock as an experiment. Still not sure about this; maybe I'm feeding feral animals, but there's not much of it and it seems to disappear. For some reason, the local wildlife doesn't like oranges.

Despite my vigilance, the occasional trip to the local tip is necessary. And I rather look forward to those trips. Weird, yes, but I am on the proverbial couch.

The local Waste Transfer Station is not a euphemism. The garbos at the station (waste managers?) do everything to ensure that stuff that can be used again *is* used again.

The first stop at the tip is a bank of container slots for cans and bottles—clear glass, brown and green glass, aluminium cans, steel cans, milk containers, clear plastics and other plastics. Sorting bottles feels a little like a kid pushing wooden shapes into a box. It's fun. Almost.

There is a dedicated space for old white goods, a pile for metals, another for timbers and a huge one for green waste. There's a basket for chemical containers and, somewhere, a drain for chemicals. There's a place for cardboards and paints and, at the far end of the tip, there's the Corner of Shame—a pile of mattresses. It costs you $70 to drop a mattress at the tip but, even though you pay for it, the garbos are never happy to see them in the back of your ute.

The garbos take their job seriously. They will peer into the back of your ute and reel off what goes where and, inevitably, say, 'The rest goes into the pit.' They say this with disappointment, because the pit is what they try to avoid. It's all the stuff that can't be recycled, all the junk that ends up in landfill. Every time I have to toss stuff into the smelly concrete pit, I feel their disapproval.

It *is* weird to be so focused or obsessed with rubbish. But you either deal with it diligently and intelligently or you foul your house and your land. I'm not as diligent when in Sydney. Those trucks that visit every week make me lazy in the city. But I'm better than I used to be because I've been forced to get close and smelly with my own waste on the land.

There are studies on the psychology of waste. A major takeaway is how forcing people to eyeball a problem or handle it themselves is a great deterrence to the creation of waste—no doubt they use that expression 'lived experience'. Giving waste a value or another purpose also helps, even if it's just giving your rotten carrots another opportunity as compost. I'm not sure there's a study on people who become obsessed with rubbish; if there is, I'm not sure I want to read it.

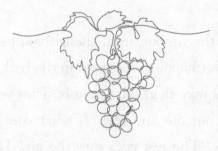

2 0

Show and Tell Too Much

We are about to meet Alex, our winemaker. Or, to be more correct, he is coming to our vineyard for an inspection that will determine whether or not he becomes our winemaker.

I'm not sure who is inspecting whom or what he wants to inspect. He might want to count the vines or, more likely, check the maturity of the vines and whether they're old enough to produce decent grapes. Perhaps he will be checking for herbicide use—a touchy subject in the area and one on which many winemakers are making a stand. He'll probably want to see how we've trained the vines. He might kick over some soil. He might want to see how rich our farm looks, so he can adjust his fees accordingly. He'll be disappointed there. He might want to check out the stories he may have heard around town about the amateurs on the Hill.

It's hard to prepare for such a visit, especially as he didn't give us any indication of what he wanted to see and we didn't know how to explain what we want of him. It's a bit like meeting the in-laws. You want to create a good impression, but you have to be on the alert.

So, I make a lemon slice.

He arrives on a cloudy winter morning. And a busy one for the farm. In the shearing shed, Ian is making another shearing stand because the shearing contractor has said he doesn't want to send out a team of shearers if they can only use two stands. Patrick is on a quick visit to the shed to check on the sheep and chat with Ian. Around the back of the Hill, a team of wood choppers in three trucks is making the most of the dead trees that dot the bald scalp of the Hill.

After bumping elbows with Alex, we're unsure where to begin. Roger starts talking about the last few years in the vineyard and his enthusiasm for the project is apparent, but

I'm not sure how Alex is responding. Alex is quietly spoken and seems often to be over-spoken by Roger's enthusiasm.

Roger takes him through some of the trials we've experienced establishing the vineyard—the cyclone, the dry, various storms—and still Alex remains aloof. Momentarily I wonder if Alex is thinking our vineyard is cursed or if he is hard of hearing, but finally I ask him what he wants to know about the vineyard and he tells us.

Evidently trunk rot is a thing. 'It's good that your vines are young, because you can prune to prevent it,' he says. We haven't heard about this rot, but then nor have most of the growers in the area, because it has only been studied —and partly solved—in the last year or so.

Alex tells us that some forms of winter pruning can allow rot into the wounds and it travels unnoticed down the trunk for a decade or so before finally killing the vine. For once, we feel clever for being the newest kid on the block.

Alex is in favour of cane-pruning rather than spur-pruning. We know cane-pruning means you take most of the growth off the vines so that the new season's growth is more vigorous. I'm not sure what other advantages it offers. Spur-pruning allows most of the lateral growth and the tips of the vertical canes in place. Instinctively, Roger and I are reluctant to cut off all the growth that we have so carefully managed over the past few years. It feels a bit like shaving

140

your head because you have lice. I don't think Alex is going to talk us into cane-pruning.

We talk about viticulture and the state of our vines and the weather; Alex remains reticent. There are long stretches of silence, and Roger and I are both thinking the same thing: maybe he doesn't want to be our winemaker but he's too polite to say so. Maybe he's going to back away slowly, hop into his ute, bolt down the driveway and we'll never see him again. Alex is really hard to read.

So it surprises both of us when he suddenly pipes up, 'We can make some good wine from this.'

We take a moment to take this in. We've got a winemaker! We're going to make wine. It's happening. I wish Roger and I could do a dance, but Alex would not be impressed with that. He might slink away while we're mid-tango.

After another (strained) half hour, we take off to inspect his winery, which is at the other end of the valley and isn't open to tourists. 'Prosaic' is how Alex describes it. And it looks like a working shed.

It looks like the sort of winery we used to visit in the 1980s in the Hunter Valley. At that time, tastings were done in sheds or in lean-to buildings at the side of the road. You'd pull up in a car, wander into a shed or roadside shelter and wait for the owner to wander out, get behind a trestle table and whip out a few bottles. It was basic, but the price of the wine was cheaper—like fruit from a roadside stand—and you'd get to chat with the person who made it.

But around that time, winemakers discovered there was money in tourism—perhaps more money in tourism than in their bottles. Now they are architect-designed destinations, with food, tours, seminars, private tastings, accommodation, luxe camping and shops with cheese and picnic stuff. They have merch—just like a rock concert. I sometimes wonder at what point the vineyard becomes decoration for the tourism. More valuable as backdrop than crop.

Alex's winemaking shed has none of this and, as we wander in and squeeze past giant metal vats, I struggle to know what to ask.

'My, they're big tanks, aren't they?' We don't say that. 'My, they're big plastic buckets, aren't they?' We do say that and discover that the buckets—Nally bins—are what we put the grapes in during harvest.

Alex shows us how much of our expected harvest (about 400 litres this year) will fit into one of his tanks. He points to a medium-sized tank and his hand goes down, down, until he has to bend his knees and show that our grape juice will only fill the bottom eighth of the tank.

Do we feel small? Yep. Do we feel like we're wasting his time? Yep. Am I thinking that this amount of wine won't fill a Christmas list of presents for friends? Yep. And then he shows us a much smaller tank. Our juice will just fill one of those. We'll be the baby in the winery.

Apart from the metal tanks, there is a room full of French oak barrels—mostly new or a few years old. A few of the recently arrived barrels have the stamp of Louis Latour on them. We're in good company here. I wonder whether our wine will have a brief stay in a Louis Latour barrel—that's almost as exciting as spending a few weeks in a chateau. Alex explains that he knows the cooper for the Louis Latour estate in France and he has bought some other barrels made by him (without the Latour insignia and therefore cheaper).

Listening to him speak about the barrels, I can't help running my hands over the smooth wooden curve of a barrel and imagining all the wines that have come out of similar barrels over the centuries. Millennia, in fact, because *Wine101* tells me they were originally used in the first century after the Romans moved through France.

So the Romans drank wine from barrels just like these. Knights of the Middle Ages imbibed from something similar after their crusades. The royal families of England, the Lancasters and the Yorks, and Henry VIII would have toasted each other with wine from barrels. Popes may have poisoned people with wine from barrels. They were even stowed on the First Fleet sailing to Australia—although those barrels were full of tar. (If the French had made it to our shores a littler earlier, I bet their barrels wouldn't have been full of tar.) Our wine might only be in an oak barrel for a few weeks but, for that period, all our labour, all our hopes and all our mistakes would be part of an ancient tradition.

When we walk out of the winery, my feet are numb with the cold and my mind is spinning with information overload. I want to feel excited, but I am trying to remember everything we've discussed.

Trunk rot. It's a thing, but we can prune to protect against it.

Herbicide. It's an issue we need to address and make a decision soonish. I'm against its use and Roger is wondering whether he can use it just one more season so he doesn't have to spend weeks swinging a whipper-snipper under the grow line.

Soil boosters. A seaweed mixture is good for the foliage, so too is another bio-something mixture that was mentioned. I wonder if it's possible to boost soil that has been depleted by herbicide.

We should decide how we're going to get our grapes from field to winery. Best idea is to drive to winery, get them to load ute with giant plastic box (I now know they're called Nally bins) and drive it back to vineyard.

Picking time. Probably mid-March, but we need to keep checking with Alex. It could be an early harvest or a late one; there could be a traffic jam at the winery at that time, so that might affect the delivery of our grapes to their new home. I hope I'm still on good terms with our kids and my brothers and sisters in mid-March when the call to pick is made.

Labels should be completed early. He mentions this a few times, because on too many occasions freelance winegrowers like us have turned up at his winery with their Nally bins full of fruit but no labels to slap on the bottles.

One wraparound label or two labels? Must decide.

Information that must be included on labels can be found on the Wine Australia site. There is still dispute with the government about the pregnancy warning.

Think about whether we need printing on the bottle caps. Really?

Think about printing on the cartons. No way, we'll just slap a label on them.

Sunscreen. Not for us, but for the grapes. It's a thing. And I think Alex is in favour of it.

Spraying for mould. Buy sprayer soon. Start spraying early. We may need to spray every few weeks from November till the nets go on in January.

Nets. Ahhhh. I do not want to think about how we get nets over the vines or (and this is meant to be the hard part) off the vines.

When we get back to the farm, we share the lemon slice that I forgot to offer Alex. I realise that a deal has been done, but no paperwork was exchanged. In fact, I don't think we even shook on it. Alex had just said he'd make the wine; he mentioned a modest fee in a roundabout way, and we left it at that. I guess that's the way deals are struck in the country—with a nod and a good-oh, but with nary a document in sight.

I decide we have time to plant the gum trees I bought yesterday. These four trees must bring the total number of natives planted to 140-odd (not including the dearly departed). It would be so much simpler if we could just be tree growers.

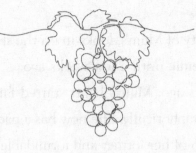

21

Succession: Too Soon and Not Soon Enough

I'm staring at the sheep that have gathered around the paddock nearest to the house and turned their backs on me as I drive past. I get a view of their bums. Are their bums too poo-ey? That is, are they normal, slightly shitty bums—or are they fly-struck? Do they need a decent rain shower to clean them up, or are they being eaten alive from the inside?

Mum wonders why I don't have much interest in sheep, and I'm thinking of her as I look at them. I've heard gossip (okay, it was Mary) that Mum would like me to take more interest in the sheep on the Hill. At the moment, Roger and I look after the vineyard, and Patrick, who manages another property of Mum's, looks in on the sheep. Suits me. This was academic until a few weeks ago.

A few weeks ago, Mum's heart started failing. And I'm not talking metaphorically. She now has a pacemaker and is regaining much of her former and formidable energy. None of us want to dwell on what might have been.

Mum almost died. Her heart rate was dangerously low, it was erratic. She collapsed at home. She was first taken to the local hospital, then into Canberra. Emergency surgery.

Waiting. First, for hours. Then for a day. To see if everything was going to be all right. It turned out everything was going to be all right, but there is an unbearable emptiness while you're waiting to hear whether someone you love has died. I breathed lightly, as if I couldn't be too greedy in my living-ness while my mother hovered near death. As if I didn't deserve that much breath if my mother had none. Share it around, treasure it, go lightly in this life. I don't know.

A few weeks on, we now pretend that it was just a hiccup. Like a flu. Or a kidney stone. Everything is back to normal. Except my confidence. And maybe Mum's confidence. Possibly the sheep's confidence.

After our shock and fear had subsided, we all asked ourselves the same question. What would have happened?

There are (and don't hold me to these numbers) about nine farms, probably twenty properties, about 12,000 livestock (and multiplying fast after the drought), about half-a-dozen full-time or part-time workers, a dozen regular contractors, three or four town businesses and a vineyard.

Obviously, Mum has also been wondering what might have happened and what she would like to happen if a hiccup re-occurs. While she's not about to cede control, she is talking about sharing information and knowledge. I suspect she'd like to educate me on fly-struck sheep bums.

It might be time.

She's eighty-nine years old. Ray is ninety-one years old. Most people would say: it's about time. But I've always thought that if they are still capable and interested in running a farming empire then they should. The problem with that is that if they were both to die while still controlling the management and information of all their enterprises then they would leave a bloody big mess behind. And the mess would be ours to muddle through.

But, perhaps worse than that, the children who might be interested in taking up ownership and management of various parcels of land would be incapable of doing so. They'd be like me, staring at the bums of sheep and wondering if there is such a thing as sheep bum wipes. And whether they are available in the supermarket.

Mum wants many of us to take over her landholdings, to embed ourselves in the farming life. To carry on her . . . well, not her legacy so much as her love of the land. And to do that effectively, I think she needs to hand over some of those duties, controls and management before she hops into an ambulance for the last ride.

Now, from my perspective, I'm not sure I want to be a sheep farmer. Just looking at those bums leaves me humming a little tune in the back of my throat. If they look nervous because I'm driving past them, how would they feel if I was in charge of them?

There are several hundred ewes out there on Cockatoo Hill, and they will soon be joined by hundreds of cute little lambs. And there's a fox living down near the creek. And the wool around their bums is getting dirty. And in the next few months their woolly coats will have to be removed by who-knows-who and taken to market, which is God-knows-where, by someone with a big truck. That's the sum of my knowledge.

Succession is complicated. It always is on the land, but even more when there are so many children, grandchildren and properties.

I remember telling Mum recently—it might have been just after her health hiccup—'Mum, I want to farm with you.' I choked when I said it. I'm not sure whether that's because I want to learn to farm under her guidance, or that I don't want to farm without her, or that she should not die soon because I am not ready for it and I want to continue to deny the possibility. I think what I meant was that I want to be a farmer on my own land—on this land—but I want to do it alongside her.

I don't feel confident enough yet to farm the land after Mum has gone. I want to know that this land will be mine and then grow it, develop it, nurture it with Mum by my side. I want to show her what I've done so she can put it on her fridge door.

Succession is tough. Just ask the royals of England and Europe, or the business moguls of today or the lawyers that are inevitably involved. It's difficult for both sides, but I suspect it's harder for those ceding control. I keep telling myself, and reminding Roger, that we must approach our work on the farm as a pastime, a hobby, a lesson, a diversion from city life. That is, we have to enjoy the process, without a sense of entitlement about the outcome. We might have to walk away with nothing but memories. And we need to be happy about that because we wouldn't want to be bitter at this stage of our life.

In the meantime, I can still look at the sheep on the Hill and think: *Umm, their bums look dirty, I must tell Mum.* We can still look out at the flock from the kitchen window while we're having breakfast and wonder why they're moving from one paddock to another, and come to our own ignorant conclusions. Do they want to go to a sunnier side? More grass? Better-tasting grass? Change of scenery? Is the grass always greener . . .

I just had a call from Mum. She was ringing to say she liked my column in the paper today (I'm on the fridge door!). We talked of the imminent rain; about why she's selling wethers rather than keeping them for wool (lamb prices versus wool prices, and fear of the Chinese trade war). About when Ian is going to get around to repairing the driveway; whether she should buy a major piece of equipment before the end of the tax year. And then she mentions that the sheep are going to be crutched this week.

Shitty bums? I ask. Mum explains that they're not fly-struck yet, but their bums are getting messy so they need the wool to be removed. I don't say 'I thought so', but I feel a flush of smugness.

After the call ends, I realise that she is teaching me about sheep care. She is passing on the information I will need after she's gone. And I am curious about sheep care. The transition may be underway. Whether I like it or not. Whether I realise it or not. And whether the sheep like it or not.

22

A Feast for the Apocalypse

Winter pruning. We're in the original vineyard. It's three-and-a-half years old already and we think we might get a harvest from it early next year. Richard, the viticulturalist, has suggested we could make wine from the sangiovese, but to leave the shiraz for another year and leave the riesling for a year or two. I suspect there will be more demand for sango too, given it's a rarer grape variety and more fashionable.

Richard teaches us how to spur-prune, leaving two small buds at the base of last year's arching canes—buds that will turn into grape bunches. Or do they turn into new canes? Must pay attention.

Vines are robust, and yet buds are tender. A brush with a glove and you've lost your bunch of grapes. Worse, you've lost a glass of wine. Pruning is all about shaping the vine for what you want to produce. You're looking for the buds that will become bunches of grapes, but also for the canes that will shoot up and form a canopy over the grape bunches—a canopy that will be managed with wires so the shade of the leaves falls on the bunches in ways both to promote growth and ripening and also to protect them from sunburn.

Older, more experienced hands can imagine what the late summer vine will look like when they snip around the bare branches in winter. I find it hard. Buds the size of a freckle becoming bunches of grapes? And where are the beginnings of those canes that may be finger thick by the end of summer? The bare bones of a vine in winter give little clue to the fecundity that lies ahead.

❧

Our fingers are cold and stiff as we begin work around 8 am on a day that starts at 7 degrees and won't get much beyond 10 degrees.

Toby is helping us and I wonder if he can see the grapes in the buds. He is wearing headphones, listening to music.

Part of me thinks he's got the right idea. I'd love to do a playlist for growing grapes (I'm thinking Queen's 'We Are the Champions'), but the sounds of the birds and the sounds of country waking up to another day are music enough.

For some reason I begin thinking of the Romans again. How they claimed land with grape vines. Annexation via cultivation. Roger says he's heard that Romans only conquered lands where they could grow grapes. Evidently, they not only drank the wine but used it on wounds as an antiseptic and as a pain killer during surgery. I hope our grapes are more than medicinal.

Besides, I suspect the Romans didn't run out of ambition just because they ran out of wine country. They didn't storm into a new territory and check out the terroir before erecting tents. They simply ran out of puff, or started fighting with each other. The Visigoths may have descended. Or the hubris of empire may have caught up with them. There's a clue in those murals of Roman emperors and their court lying around on cushions, dribbling grapes into their mouth while nubile virgins (or once-were-virgins) drape themselves over the portly men. Sloth, indolence and grapes! They really liked grapes.

Brooke is helping us today. She tells us that her husband and she have shut their hatted restaurant in town, and they are planning to open a sourdough bakery. We lose their restaurant but gain a bakery. I'm not sure how I feel about that, but I think we won out of that contest.

Wine and bread—what more would we need? Lamb for celebrations. About five hundred of them are about to be born on the Hill—that's 2000 legs of lamb there. There's a fig tree too in the corner of the garden. This is looking more like a Roman assemblage in my imagination.

Roger has started talking about whether the Hill could be an escape from the world. He asks what sort of vegetables we could grow. Potatoes? he asks. He's looking to fill out the plate of roast lamb.

No, I reply, I don't think this land is suitable for potatoes. Carrots?

Maybe, I say, thinking of the rabbits that burrow in the hillside and how much they'd love a crop of carrots.

We could grow stone fruits, I suggest. Peaches, apples, quince, but probably not citrus. Brussels sprouts would do well, I tease.

We're being silly, pretending we're preparing for an apocalypse. But are we being silly? The media is full of stories of self-sufficiency as Covid sweeps the globe. People in many parts of the world are asking the same question—are we surrounded by the sort of assets that could sustain us through a collapse in supply chains, social order or even a blip in the digital functioning of the modern world?

Assets? A story I read used this word, but these wouldn't be the usual assets, the ones that make it onto a balance sheet. Money would still count, but not as much as it did last year, and maybe not as much as next year. In a post-apocalyptic world, an inventory of assets would look very different to the 2019 one. Trading would be more important than cash reserves. A house with a water view would not be worth as much as a house with a water supply. A house with a parterre garden wouldn't be worth as much as a house with dead trees for firewood. A garage of fancy cars wouldn't be worth as much as a store of petrol—diesel and regular—and a good lock for the fuel shed.

Jobs and bosses would be worth less than friends with skills. A field of food and a community to trade with would top the list. Knowing how to fix machinery would be as highly prized as fixing a broken bone, and far higher than fixing a smile. And you'd need a supply of old wires, timbers and metals so you could improvise repairs. Shit, I shouldn't have cleaned up all that junk.

Calculating for the apocalypse is sobering, even with a vineyard in view, and we're not the only ones quietly catastrophising. In *The New York Times* there's a piece prompting the boomers to get back to the core business of the sixties: 'The hippie back-to-the-land movement, combined with grassroots political organising really was the way to go. We need to regroup. We need a hyperlocal Green New Deal. We need to come together in diverse, intimate, place-based communities. And we need to segue now from the techno-industrial market economy to its sequel— much smaller-scale, less energy-intensive, more localised communities that prize food growing, knowledge sharing, inclusiveness and convivial neighbourliness.' Maybe we *could* grow potatoes.

We're not the only ones in Australia seeking solace in wine, bread and country living. Stories in the real estate sections have been tracking the movements of people during the pandemic. In the US and Australia, and I suspect elsewhere, people are moving out of the city centres. Some are hugging the edges of cities in suburbs; others are moving further out, mostly up and down the coast.

But some are going regional—two-, three- or four-hour commutes from a major city. That is, if you could call that a commute. Once you're that far out, the city is no longer a commute. It's a holiday destination; it's a visit to family and friends. More people will cast their eyes to the regions, to the land, to the place where bread, wine and country living become possible. Imperative, even.

I'm losing perspective. But, in these dark days of 2020's isolation and immobility, there's time to recalibrate. To wonder. There's time to ponder whether a broken-down house can accommodate all your children and their partners. To tote up what skills they could bring to the countryside. Designing, communicating, writing, strong hands, sharp-shooting . . .

Oh no, I've gone too far. Surely we won't need sharp-shooting for anything except foxes, rabbits and dying sheep. Would we really have to put a gun on the list? Near the top of the list? We're not hillbillies. We don't want to turn ourselves into those antisocial people who retreated to the wild hills of America and kept watch for intruders while sitting on their balconies with a gun resting on their laps.

Perhaps the children can make sourdough and we'll make wine. Maybe we could clandestinely locate a gin still up the Hill (there's the hillbilly again). A crop of marijuana—medicinal of course. And figs.

God bless the person who planted a fig tree in the garden so long ago. And there's an olive tree too that I have just remembered. Lamb, olive oil, bread, figs and (if a pig is traded) prosciutto too. We're sounding very Roman.

Sometimes, you have too much time to think. I smack my hands together to get blood flowing. I should give myself a smack around the cheeks. And not just for blood flow.

We don't know how this will end, how it will progress even. Besides, these buds—these tiny furry buds that get knocked off by clumsy hands—won't become wine for another year. Hold that thought.

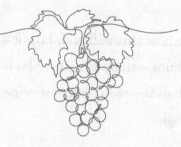

23

Do My Underpants
Look Big Here?

Friends are coming to visit. They're good friends so I'm looking forward to welcoming them. But they're also sophisticated and used to the best of everything.

When I visit their homes I marvel at their renovations, their art collection and the fact that they have the best of everything. I even envy their garden hose. So much so that I bought a hose just like their hose, if only because it was the only thing that was the best of the best that I could afford. I hate the hose: it's way too heavy. I drag it around the garden like a firefighter. It seemed so perfect in their place, but in mine . . .

They are great people. Decent people. I really get along with them. But, when they first arrive at the farm, I feel like I'm not wearing underpants. I'm not a jealous person. I'm not a status person—well not much—and I'm not often fussed about what people think of me. So, what's going on? Why do I feel stripped bare by their arrival?

Okay, obviously it's the asbestos dosshouse that worries me. I was shocked and horrified when I first saw it; so I know they're going to be just as shocked.

Really? You invited us to travel 300 kilometres to visit this shack? Can we get asbestos disease just by walking past it? Don't tell me you're going to invite us inside.

That's what I imagine them thinking as they park their smart European car (now covered with dust from the driveway, which frankly is a disgrace even to country people, who know how important having a gravel driveway is).

They're polite. Of course, they are. I usher them around the outside of the decrepit part of the house and into the slightly liveable part of the house; I open the warped back door and the flyscreen door that is slightly flappable, and I proudly point out the new wood burner. I am thrilled by the wood burner. It's only a few weeks old and emits that warm-me-to-the-bones feeling that no electric heating system could ever replicate.

'This is cosy,' they say. Yeah, like a bear's cave is cosy. Or a wombat's burrow. Or a gypsy's caravan.

I'm making excuses now. 'It's really just a crash pad for us,' I say. 'I can't wait to demolish that horrible part of the house. I close my eyes every time I walk past those broken windows and flaking asbestos panels and pipes that go nowhere.' I prattle on.

I have a fire pit set up on the lawn overlooking the vineyard, because people from the city expect a fire pit. Champagne is chilling. Some cheese. And fancy sausages. 'Look there are newborn lambs in the paddock! Do you want to see the century-old shearing shed? Or the new holding pens?'

The weekend is already exhausting and I want to bash myself up. *Why do you care, Deirdre? What are you afraid of? What were you bloody thinking of, inviting such stylish people to your hilltop shack?*

Okay, it is an I-forgot-to-wear-underpants moment and any moment I will trip over and they will see that I'm not wearing them. Or they've got holes in them. Or they're like the underpants Mum used to sew for us when we were too poor for Bonds. Underpants made from the same fabric as our school uniforms—voluminous and wrong.

❧

But there was something else going on. And I only realised it later, when I was back in Sydney in my well-built house with the fancy garden hose: I was afraid of them seeing me in a new light. My emergent self.

That sounds clinical, but I like it because it sounds like I'm an alien. I think it means that I'm a different person down on the farm to who I am in Sydney. I'm rehearsing a new version of myself. A person who likes different things, who feels differently about life. A person who feels comfortable in the country, who doesn't automatically wear a bra, who can look at hands of busted fingernails and think, *Maybe they'll grow again in winter.* A farmer? Nah, that's too soon.

I think I was nervous about their response because I'm not yet confident about this new me. If they had turned around and said, 'Cut it out, Deirdre, you don't like this stuff' or 'You can't do this' or 'Who do you think you're kidding?', I'd have curled up into a ball and shouted, 'I know, I know.' Sometimes I can hear myself saying the same thing to myself: 'Who do you think you're kidding? Pretend farmer, pretend winegrower. Put your work gloves away and get a manicure.'

They were probably not thinking anything like that. But I can't help thinking about the idea of seeing yourself through the eyes of others. That's where we draw much of our identity, even if we don't admit it. Our identity is shaped, or at least whittled, by how others respond to us.

165

Are we feared? Then, we must be fearsome. Are we liked? We must be nice. Are we treated with respect? That's my favourite—we all need to be respected as equal humans, especially women. Other people are our mirrors; we read in their faces what they see in us and that becomes part of us.

We're social animals, so the social is important. There are books on behavioural science that prove the impact our social network has on our moods, our weight, our bad habits, our good habits. Social contagion theory tells us that our behaviour is as much to do with whom we call our friends as how we want to behave. It says our identity is as malleable as our brains are plastic.

I'm beginning to flex my way into a new outfit, but I'm used to people seeing me in my old identity. I know what to expect from that social identity; they know what to expect from that identity. I'm not sure about this new person. My rabbit-felt hat feels a little wobbly now. My steel-capped boots a bit over-the-top. The pants with lots of pockets and hooks are too try-hard. If they don't call my bluff, I might.

The weekend went well. We built a fire, ate sausages, visited my Mum, walked up the Hill, saw some lambs, ate dinner at a fine restaurant and played golf the next day.

I don't think the driveway damaged their car. I took them though the decrepit part of the house and they didn't freak out. I didn't trip over and expose my homemade underpants.

But I'm unnerved by my reaction to their visit.

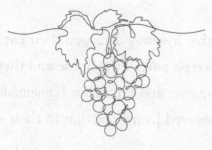

24

Betsy, Zoe and Parsley Arrive

The morning reverie is broken by the sound of a ute barrelling up the driveway and crunching to a stop near the shearing shed. Dogs bark and, as a door of the ute bangs shut, the sound of swearing pierces our open bedroom window.

'Patrick's arrived,' I say. Even Roger, slightly hard of hearing, clocked that.

The dogs are keen to get to work on the sheep that are crammed into the holding pens adjacent to the shearing shed. The pack rounded them up from around the Hill yesterday and clearly they think their work isn't finished. Patrick, in so many swear words, tells them that today is not the day for mustering.

It can be scary overhearing Patrick yell commands at his dogs, especially as his orders usually start with 'f-ing' and end with a worse swearword. But then you hear the names of the dogs he is shouting at. His dogs have pretty names, courtesy of Patrick's partner, Jana. Among them are Parsley, Zoe and Betsy. So the profane commands lose some of their menace when directed at a herb.

Watching Patrick and his dogs round up the flock yesterday was like watching a dance across the landscape. As he sped around the sheep paddocks on the quad bike, I had expected something like a herding of cats, a day-long exercise in chasing down errant sheep and terrorising the herd into smaller and smaller paddocks. But with his three dogs and quad bike it took Patrick less than an hour to muster hundreds of sheep into the holding pens.

The dogs were masters at mustering. They seemed to know exactly what to do. I don't know how they do that. Sure, Patrick yells commands at them, but how do dogs translate a few profane directions into action? Are they born that way? What do they really think 'f-ing' means?

Patrick, a local from a big family, grew up with sheep and dogs and fast farm vehicles. He is fearless in the paddocks and a sweetie in company. But today he might have something more challenging on the agenda.

Within minutes of Patrick's arrival, a retinue of utes sweeps up the driveway to the shearing shed. It's the shearing crew. I peek out the window as the crew of six swaps greetings, lights up cigarettes and settles dogs in the trays of utes. The crew members don't tarry for long. Just after 7 am, they're in the shed, where a ritual as old as colonial settlement begins.

The running of the shearing shed hasn't changed much since unions got involved in the nineteenth century. The rules are known to all; the chain of command is respected by all. It all begins with the shearing contractor.

I'd accompanied Mum on the day when the contractor came and made suggestions about fixing up the shed to make it fit for the crew. I've never seen Mum fix up a place so fast. The stairs into the shed needed replacement— about two decades ago—and they were quickly remedied. The handrails too had to be replaced. The junk that had accumulated inside was cleared out. A working fridge was rescued and plugged in. The holding pens inside the shed were reconfigured so shearers didn't have to duck under wooden beams.

Mum promised to install another permanent stand, so three shearers could operate at once. A new door was installed into the side of the shed so the bales of wool could be tipped onto the back of a truck. The bench where the

170

brown snake used to live was cleared out (I'm not sure the contractor knew about the snake).

There are lots of rules around the shearing shed, some of which are centuries old and have never been challenged. One of the key ones is that the owner of the property, the cocky, can be present but shouldn't interfere with the shearing. For the period of shearing, the shed is the domain of the shearers, especially the contractor.

The other rules relate to the smooth procession of the sheep to the clippers, because shearers are paid per sheep shorn and they don't stand for anything that interrupts the flow of the flock. The sheep must be corralled into the holding pens in a way that ensures the shearers don't have to reach far to grab one. The roustabout needs to keep the floors clear of wool, dags, shit, dust and whatever else comes off the wool. The classer needs to keep up with the shearers, throwing the fleeces onto the skirting table as soon as they leave the back of the sheep.

The fleeces are sorted into various cubicles, depending on their quality and cleanliness, and then put into the press to be baled. Most teams have runs of two hours of work. There are four of these runs a day and the breaks between those runs are the times when the cocky (or the cocky's daughter) can offer them cake.

I had baked a slice in Sydney and bought it down for the shearers. I remembered Mum doing that years ago and it seemed like a nice thing to do. But I lost my nerve. Walking into a shed in full action, with heavy rock turned up loud, with shouting and lots of grunts and the sound of hoofs slapping the floor, and with the stare of the wool classer taking in the newcomer, I just wanted to run. Instead of handing out the slice I had in a plastic bag, I sidled up to Patrick and asked a few inane questions as I sheltered under his 190 centimetre, 120 kilo frame.

Patrick was representing the cocky that day and he was a fine choice, and not just because of his size. He had sheared for about a decade, he knew sheep, he knew shearers and he knew when someone was taking out a bad mood on a ewe.

In a previous shearing season, Patrick had overheard a couple of shearers belittling Stefan my brother-in-law (and his father-in-law) for mistaking a ewe for a wether. Stefan attracts these sorts of comments because he is from old Czechoslovakia and, even though he knows his ewes from his wethers—and, by the by, has four degrees and really should be addressed as 'Doctor'—his accent ruffles some.

Patrick had been miffed at the shearers' ridicule so, when Stefan left the shed briefly, Patrick sidled up to them and told them to talk more quietly, because Stefan had been in the Red Army in Czechoslovakia and had been in charge of taking dissidents into a forest, forcing them to dig a ditch, lining them up along the ditch and shooting them. When Stefan returned to the shed, the shearers kept their heads down and their mouths shut.

This season's shearing must be watched closely because the crews aren't as experienced as in previous years. The pandemic has cut shearer numbers and every sheep farmer is scrambling to secure a crew. Word is that a few of the established farmers in the area have been unable to secure shearers. Word is they were the cockies who were least pleasant to the crews in previous years.

These are just comments overheard around the back of utes. A diplomatic member of the farming community wouldn't spread such gossip, so I won't. Let's just say Mum got the crews for her flocks. Maybe her cakes of previous seasons did the trick.

After ten minutes I retreated from the shed to watch the sheep as they emerged from the chute, clean-shaven and so happy with their haircuts that they did a little jig of joy as they escaped up the Hill. Inside, the bales were piling up in a corner and, as the wool was fine merino, each bale was worth more than $3000, possibly as much as $4000. It has been a good year for wool; not as solid as the previous year, but getting better as the year progresses. It's not a bad year for living on the land, or off it, for many reasons.

As I ambled back to the shack, thinking of fine woollen suits with European labels and appreciating anew the wool socks I'd been wearing for two days, I kicked myself for not leaving the slice for the crew. But it feels fake. I'm no cocky's wife and I'm not sure I want to perpetuate the stereotype. The tradition of shearing might have been regaled in song, paintings, poems and politics for most of settlement, but it doesn't need me as handmaiden.

I also chide myself for not asking more questions. Especially of the classers, who can determine a micron rating from the fling of a fleece. But I console myself that I was able to steer the women in the crew to the better bathroom at the habitable end of the house, so they didn't have to face the bathroom in the dosshouse.

2 5

Dumpsville Revisited

It takes a while to inhabit a house. You have to walk its floors; breathe in its spaces; wipe its surfaces with care, with love even. You need to sleep in peace and make food there; to invite friends in; fill its chambers with talk; warm it on winter nights and manage the summer heat with careful curtaining. You bring your life to a house and, slowly, the house comes to life. But it's not just about you. The house has to let you in.

The half of the house where we stay now feels like a part of us. We have routines that begin with a cup of tea in bed and finish with a gaze at the star-bright sky through the bedroom window. We know its weak spots—from the way bowing floorboards create a feeling of walking uphill to the toilet flusher that you must keep pressing for the duration of the flush. And we thank it for its best spots—the winter sun that bathes the lounge room, the morning view across a foggy paddock, the birdsong that breaks the dawn, the setting sun that turns dust motes pink. It's only four rooms and a bathroom, but it's enough.

The other part of the house is like a nightmare that lingers in a waking moment. Unsettling, but soon forgotten. For four years now I have tried to forget it's there. I walk past it with my eyes averted so I won't see the cracked windows, shaky asbestos walls and the offensive scale of too many cheap, ill-conceived additions. If I have to walk through the old part, I keep the doors closed and try not to breathe deeply, cursing the fact that it's there. I curse it a lot actually. As if it is to blame for its exhausted fittings, its skanky carpet, mouldy ceilings and the 1940s kitchen still furnished with kettle, mugs, crockery, two cookers (one of which is wood powered) and a rusting hulk of a fridge that I'm too scared to open.

It looks haunted. But I try not to dwell on that because, if I start thinking it's haunted, I wouldn't be able to walk past, much less walk in the back door. Or sleep. When I wake to strange sounds in the middle of the night, I try to tell myself that it's a branch falling or a bat taking a wrong path or a mouse in search of dinner. But I inevitably think it's the return of the serial killer that I'm certain resided here at some stage.

It has occurred to me that the old part of the house is, in fact, haunted, but only because I fill it with my foul thoughts. I have cast a curse on it; I have given it that cursed character and it's reflecting that back. I'm the ghost.

※

A few weekends ago, something shifted. It was when I was farewelling the plumber and the tiler who had been working on the inhabited part of the house. I mentioned they might come back one day and strip out the 1980s bathroom in the slightly liveable part of the house. The plumber thought I meant the bathroom in the haunted section.

'Oh no,' I said, 'that part of the house should be condemned, and one day I hope to bulldoze it and build a new section.'

'There's a lot you could do to fix it up, you know,' Jim the plumber said. 'It's a solid house. All the structures are sound. I think it could be a pretty little house.'

The tiler quickly concurred, adding that, because it was fibro, walls could be moved around, windows replaced.

They'd both had a look around while they were working on the newer part of the house. I wondered why they were interested. Sure, they may have wanted to drum up more work, but they seemed genuine. It was the first time I'd heard anyone, except Mum, talk well of the house.

It was shortly after this that I took my city friends on the haunted house tour. They too thought the house could be rescued. 'It's a country cottage,' one of them had said. 'Why not keep it like that, rather than build something that might not fit so well?'

I started to look at the old house with new eyes. Kinder eyes. When my friends left, I walked through its rooms to re-acquaint myself.

The first thing I did was check whether the floorboards, which were cut as narrow boards and looked like cedar, extended beyond the exposed floors of the hallway. They did. They were hidden under the skanky carpet of the big room and under the cracked lino of the kitchen. Something worth saving.

I stood in the kitchen and imagined a window on its eastern side, overlooking the vineyard. The outdoor laundry would have to go. No room for a big fridge, but I could figure something out.

I held my breath lightly when I stood in the bathroom. Small. Grimy, with splatter marks of mould. But workable. The jerry-built sunroom, which straddled the north side of the house, had salvaged windows set so high it could be a prison exercise space. It looked unworkable. Everything about it—from the low ceiling to the step down from the main house and the silly high windows—was wrong. Wrong. Wrong. Wrong. The room/bedroom next to it was the wrong shape. Long but narrow. More than a corridor, not quite a room. A problem.

Lately, I have been waking at night with blueprints on my mind, trying to reshape the shack into something workable, something with integrity. On recent visits I have walked the floors of the haunted house, hoping for inspiration, mentally taking its measure, idly imagining its future. And funnily, it doesn't seem as scary as it was. It just feels forgotten. Hard done by, maybe.

I'm not sure if this little cottage will ever be pretty but I do know that it's not haunted anymore. Maybe it never was. I had haunted it with my mean thoughts, with my curses.

I have started moving more junk out of the rooms (trips to the tip never end). On my next visit, I hope to lift the skanky carpets in the biggest room to reveal the floorboards. Maybe I'll run a mop over the surfaces to get rid of the smell of neglect. Rip down the plywood wardrobe and investigate what is making it smelly. Tear posters from the 1970s off the wall and hope not too much asbestos comes with them. The Batman light shade has to go. One day, this shambolic house might feel loved. And, if I love it back, it might allow us to inhabit it.

But my equanimity didn't last. My sister and I were walking out of the old kitchen when she opened the freezer door of the fridge. I'd never done this. I had opened the main door of the fridge a few years ago, just before I turned off the power, on the basis that such a hulking wreck of an appliance would be churning through too much power and was soon to be taken to the tip. It's possible I'd never opened the freezer because I didn't want to know what was in there.

Mary's idle decision to open the freezer confirmed my worst premonitions. The door was open only a few seconds before she slammed it shut but not before the foulest smell to ever visit this land gushed out of the freezer.

We bolted outside and looked at each other.

'What *was* that?' she asked.

As if I knew. As if I'd cut up the limbs of a hapless stranger and stuffed them into the freezer. We looked at each other in silence, each of us remembering scenes from horror movies that always end up with something foul in the freezer.

I don't often do this, but when I found Roger I played the too-sensitive-for-this-world female. Please remove whatever is in the freezer. I can't face it, I can't even go back into the house. Please, please.

It was fish. Probably salmon. Probably very palatable when it was placed in the freezer five or six years ago, and still palatable when I turned off the fridge three years ago. The atrociously smelly globules of decomposed fish were removed by the man of the house. The fridge was strapped shut and shuffled out of the house for the trip to the tip a few days later.

Finally, there was no corner of the house I hadn't faced. There were no more bodies under the floorboards. The ghosts were leaving.

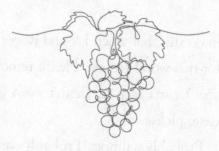

2 6

Dinner on the Hoof

It is a winter morning and I'm heading towards the shearing shed to shovel sheep droppings from the area under the holding pens. Most of the droppings are mature enough to work magic on soil. It has been months since shearing sprinkled a fresh layer of droppings through the boards, but most of the manure is years old. The fertiliser is dry, light, pleasant smelling and perfect for roses, and at this time of year I can shovel it without fear of lurking animals.

Not that I've seen a snake under the shearing shed or anywhere around the house. There have only been a couple of reptile sightings—a large black snake near the creek crossing, a small black snake slithering under a row of vines and a brown snake that Ian encountered in the upper vineyard. That was years ago but, outside the winter months, I still find myself scanning the immediate horizon for them.

Richard, the viticulturalist, still won't let me forget the day he visited the newly planted shiraz vines to advise on our progress. I was facing Roger and him, looking south I believe, and Richard said to me, 'Deirdre, slowly make your way over to us.' I don't recall him using the 'S' word but I followed his glance to the row of vines beneath us and saw the black snake, by then with its head raised and its neck/gullet/whatever puffed out in alarm.

I know what to do when you spot a snake. There's a guy who runs a snake tent at the Murrumbateman Field Days, where he commands an array of deadly snakes with a hooked rod and hessian bags as he gives advice on snake behaviour. I've heard the same drill on my two visits to the field day where I watched with morbid fascination alongside the other fairgoers. You stand still. No matter what variety of snake you encounter, no matter which direction the snake is heading, no matter how fast the snake can travel, or how rapidly its venom can kill you, you stand still. Even as an observer leaning into his snake tent, I remember thinking, *That's not going to happen.*

So when Richard calmly suggested that I walk slowly toward him, I jumped and bolted to the other side of them, all the time trying to keep an eye on the snake. It was, it should be said, travelling in the opposite direction.

Richard was disappointed. He pointed out how puffed out the neck of the snake had become since I'd leapt into the air. That's a sign of a distressed snake, he said. It's scared now, he said. Richard felt sorry for the snake as I trembled behind him.

As I amble to the shed with a shovel and rubber tub, confident I won't meet any snakes this fine winter morning, I spy Patrick under a tree at the side of the shed. When I see what he's doing, I stop still (like I'm supposed to do at a snake sighting). He sees me coming and yells a greeting, so I have to keep walking towards him, but I don't want to. Patrick has a dead lamb strung up, hanging from a tree branch, and is halfway through the process of slicing the skin from its carcass. Its head is missing; the lamb has been strung up by one leg, with its other legs splaying and its belly bulging with organs. Patrick is blood-splattered and happy as a lamb. A live one. Hannibal Lecter. That's what comes to mind. I try to quash the association as I amble, a little slower, towards Patrick.

'It broke its neck in the holding pen.' Patrick is still yelling as I approach. 'May as well get a feed out of it.'

This is the moment when I must let country practicalities overcome my city squeamishness. My city sensibility wants to get upset, to ask him what went wrong and if he rang the vet to see what could be done. Or at least suggest that the lamb is buried. Somewhere nice. With a cairn maybe.

My country sensibility is saying: Face facts, the lamb is dead, freshly dead with a good layer of meat on its bones. It had a lovely life in the paddocks and a gentler end than the other lambs who are about to be sorted, pushed onto a transporter, sent to a sales yard, pushed onto another transporter and unloaded at an abattoir. This lamb had it easy and it's now going to feed the people who looked after it during its nine months in the fields.

My stomach is still in city mode. It is roiling and I just hope Patrick doesn't slice open the lamb's belly as I amble towards the tree.

'Looks like a nice bit of lamb,' I say, pretending to be blasé.

'Yeah, I'll send you a few chops and a leg,' he replies.

'Great.' I'm sounding weak now.

Patrick doesn't stop the butchering as we talk. One of his dogs is waiting for permission to eat an organ—liver, I think. The fleece is off and I can see one of the legs that he might deliver to our doorstep. I'm not sure if I can see the chops, because I don't know what part of the lamb gives us chops. Shoulder?

Patrick is so engaged in the process of turning the animal into meat that I stay a while. It's obviously something he's done before. He handles the knife deftly and swings the carcass on its rope to meet its blade. There's a lot of gore, but also grace. And respect.

As I walk back to the house—I forget about collecting the sheep poo for the moment—I realise how much work I need to do on my city sensibilities.

I come from a city suburb where you pay more in a dog parlour than in a beauty parlour, where doggy day-care costs the same as child care and doggy couture is a thing. I have a friend who spent almost $10,000 fixing a dog who was nearing the end of its life. I know of a friend of a friend who no longer sleeps with her husband because her pooch gets jealous if hubby tries to return to the marital bed. In the city, you're not meant to call yourself a pet owner; you're a pet parent and when you talk to the dog you refer to yourself as mummy or daddy.

Country people aren't uncaring about animals—Patrick was inconsolable the day his last dog died—but their tolerance for the vagaries of life is higher. Perhaps it comes with the job of keeping animals alive until the day they are sent to die.

Some animals will die under your watch, especially lambs. Just after lambing, friends came to visit and we walked up the Hill to the peak (like Hillary). One of my girlfriends spotted a bleating lamb by itself and rushed to the rescue.

It still had its umbilical cord attached and that made a mess of my friend's cashmere jumper. She carried it to us and we fussed around it, wondering how it had become separated from the flock. We must reunite it with its mother, she said.

Roger took the lamb towards the flock and gently placed it down so it could join the mob. We stood by, encouraging it to get back to the flock, cheering it on as it wobbled on new legs towards a flock that seemed oblivious to its fate. After we'd repaired to the fire pit for a glass of wine, we congratulated ourselves on the rescue. But even then I wasn't so confident.

'It wouldn't have survived,' Mum said the next day.

'How can you be so sure,' I asked, slightly taken aback by her brusqueness.

'A lot of the ewes on the Hill are old and old ewes tend to have twins. Some are so old that they just can't feed both.'

The only other solution to a wobbly orphan on the outer with its flock is to adopt it. But no one wants a poddy lamb, because you have to bottle-feed it every few hours for at least four weeks. It never stops bleating and it really messes up your carpet.

I'm guessing it would be emotionally hard to send your poddy lamb off to market too. It might be like the rabbit that hangs around our back door, sheltering under bushes but, strangely, not digging burrows. When my brother Hugh arrived to shoot rabbits with Roger, I asked him to spare the scruffy-looking rabbit outside the back door.

Why? Because it acts like a pet, like the pet rabbits our kids had when younger. And that's what matters. The difference between being an animal husbander or a pet parent will depend on your relationship with the animal and its relationship with you. In the country, there's a thin line between something you pat and something you shoot.

Or perhaps it's just a matter of timing. That lamb that Patrick had strung up to the tree branch could well have been my pet lamb if I'd picked up that newborn on the Hill and made it a poddy lamb. But, instead, it was livestock until it took a tumble and ended up with my name on its leg.

At least both city and country people can agree that no one likes the sort of animal that will kill you one day when you're not keeping an eye out, or when the warm weather arrives before your vigilance. Or if you don't run fast enough when you spot it.

The Pantone Farmer

We are designing a label. Or rather, Roger and my daughter Kate are designing it.

This seems a little premature, given that the grapes that will fill the nicely labelled bottles have just been burnt by a late spring frost. They were just tiny, furry buds with a tinge of green, and now they are turning to dust. Other buds will appear, so we've been told. We keep checking the bare branches for signs of green.

Such hope. But we remind ourselves that there are four grape vines that were planted at least fifty years ago at the bottom of the Hill near the creek, and they have survived dozens of dry years and a few killer droughts, many frosts, plus years of inattention, and they're alive and still producing sweet grapes.

The labelling process is an act of faith. It is belief and hope that none of those adverse conditions that regularly wipe out harvests will impact the harvest this year—our first. Like many acts of farming, you proceed with the hope that the fire on the distant hill or the hailstorm on the radar or the pests on the neighbouring properties won't destroy your efforts.

But it's more than that: making a label makes it real. Even after all these years, it's hard to believe that the slivers of vines we planted—and subsequently trained and pruned and fed and watered and debudded and scooped up into the foliage wires—will produce a bottle of wine. One that will be drinkable. Saleable.

A label is like raising a flag on our territory.

The name has been agreed upon and the business name has been registered. Gang Gang: named after the gang-gang cockatoo, which is related to the name of the Hill, even if said bird may not be native to our Hill.

Disclaimer: we haven't seen a gang-gang cockatoo on the Hill yet. We thought we'd seen a few, but then someone pointed out they were galahs.

You can't have a wine called Galah. Well, you could, but it would have to be a natural wine, produced by hipsters, and it would probably be undrinkable. Still, the gang-gang cockatoo is the faunal emblem of the local area, the Australian Capital Territory.

It turns out that they mostly hang out on the other side of Canberra, towards the Snowy Mountains, but, before we knew all that, we'd registered the business name and we had grown fond of the name for the label. However, the more we investigated the name and the bird and the Hill, the less sense it made. Wine drinkers like a story with their wine; they want to feel part of the process; they want to feel good about being part of the process. At the very least, they want to pick up a bottle and get the gist of the wine, the area, the maker and the grower, and whatever dreams the grower had for the wine. In this case, they have to feel good about being part of a misunderstanding. Hey, that's a story too.

The name is contentious for other reasons. It could have connotations with the musical fad out of Korea called Gangnam Style. With a slip of the tongue, it might remind some of gang bang. That wouldn't be a good Google search word unless, of course, a porn search results in a few orders. Some biker gangs might think we're muscling into their nomenclature.

The name needs to be clarified by the addition of an image or part-image of a cockatoo on the label. Then people won't think we're rough. Or a boy band.

We find an image of the gang-gang cockatoo on a tea-towel that a friend gave us. That doesn't sound stylish, but it is an artist's image of the bird done in an Australiana style. And it's an Australian artist with links to the area. Another story to tell. So Roger contacts the artist and tries to interest her in allowing her artwork be shared with a bottle of wine. She's thinking about it.

Kate is doing the design work, researching the designers' bible of colour, the Pantone colour range, and asking lots of questions of us. What image do you want to project? What's your story? Who are you pitching the wine at? How do you think it will be sold, where will it be sold, what part of the shop will it be sold in? Are you mainly going to sell online, at the cellar door, in local bars? And then she progresses to: what personality do you want the wine to project?

Personality? The grapes are just buds. We don't even know if they're going to be wine and yet we have to pick a personality? I think about wines in general and try to describe their personality. Pinot noir is always pleasant, easy-going and, if I'm feeling rich when I buy it, elegant. Champagne is bubbly, obviously. Rieslings are seemingly friendly, but sometimes they have a bitter end. Sauvignon blanc is like the airhead at the party who can't shut up. Port is a bombastic old bloke, who's straining the buttons on his waistcoat and sprays dry biscuit whenever he disapproves of what you're saying. Weird. But Kate's questions are good ones. This is, after all, a process.

The design process begins with an image of a bird that may or may not have flown over the vineyard and it plays on the name that may prompt a few awkward questions. What will carry the design through to a charming conclusion on a label is Kate's deft hand at creating an image that embodies the product. Roger and I work through her questions, but we'll have to do a marketing degree before we can answer them correctly. I thought we were becoming farmers.

As we veer into the marketing business—we haven't even settled on the style of bottle, the cap, the position of the label on the bottle, whether to have carton designs—it occurs to me that the rest of the farming community is also confronting the world of marketing. Value-added agriculture is what the federal government is talking about. Don't just make the raw product and ship it overseas in bulk containers—make the final product in Australia. Beef that's turned into branded products with provenance, a history, a barcode of production qualities and a promise of stewardship. Fruit that isn't sold in crates but is turned into jams or sauces with links to the name of the person who picked it; chickens that come with links to videos of them free-ranging in pastures; pork that is sold with a back story of heritage and a booklet about the farmer's philosophy.

Farming is now branding, and we're all being pushed into unknown territory.

But we're primary producers. That, for some on the land, was the original attraction. Certainly, that has been the history in this sheep-farming area. It's a big pivot from letting sheep graze pasture until their fleece is long enough to shear and then sending bales off to China in a container ship. Do farmers around here want to process the wool, spin, weave and turn that fleece into leisurewear that has the right label? And the right story. Baa-baa lamb meets Lululemon.

When I hear people talk of value-added farm production, I don't immediately think economics. I imagine a gnarly farmer in a hat that has weathered too many summers, with arms that have pulled dying calves from the rear of cows and with muscled fingers ingrained with dirt; I imagine him poring over a designer's moodboard of paper textures and colour swatches to decide on his label. A production that ends with a Pantone decision.

It's a pivot, but that's where the momentum is. Grow local, grow clean and green. Use local labour, employ new technology developed by our scientists and find local businesses to turn it into something that can be put on a shelf. Capture the value for Australia.

The big X in that equation is China. Our biggest trading partner has been happy to receive our containers of primary

194

produce and we've grown complacent about that. It's so easy to ship it all off and not fuss about finishing it off. But we now realise that has left us vulnerable to international politics. The wine industry is still holding its breath over China. China can wipe out billions of dollars of wine exports if it feels like it. And if that continues, Australia won't be riding on top of a wine barrel for long.

Already the big wine companies are exploring new markets and even the smaller winemakers in our area are talking about selling their wine locally. Build more cellar doors, ramp up the online sales, create wine clubs and build relationships with local bars and restaurants that will survive an international trade war. No one is in the mood to be bullied by China; no one wants them to have power over our economy. Their price is too high, even if our losses will be huge.

I suppose, that's another skill the government wants farmers to have—to be keen observers of international relations. And they are, they are. But I'm guessing they're getting weary.

Maybe I'm just getting weary, thinking about all the decisions that should be made before those pimply buds on the vines become wine bottles on the table. When our grapes are still a promise on bare vines, it feels presumptuous to address design aspirations, economic considerations, international trade disputes and the story we should tell customers about our product. Or the personality of the wine. But I'm glad Roger and Kate are enthusiastic about it, because it's an act of faith; it's our way of declaring we've arrived and this is who we are.

2 8

A Silent Shame

In mid-spring, the fields turn gold. You don't notice it at first. If you wake at dawn and look out at the—usually foggy—morning, the vines have tips of verdant green and pastures are English green from the amount of rain and the regularity of the rain we've been getting. Then, as the sun rises, a yellow tinge develops. At first, it could be mistaken for a reflection of the sun's glow or the aftermath of too much wine the night before.

Then the yellow bursts to reveal daisies. Such sunny, happy daisies. They cover the ground for hundreds of metres, tightly packed, turning slightly towards the sun and, when you walk over them, it feels like a Mary Poppins moment. I take photos of them and think about drawing them (and therefore destroying their beauty) but I can't help thinking—are these weeds?

Capeweed, also known as Cape daisy, was introduced from South Africa and popular in garden nurseries, especially in the 1950s, until the wind picked up the seeds and spread them across the eastern states of Australia. They have turned thousands of pastures into garden displays begging for a brush with Monet and, yet, when you do an online search, the results inevitably begin with 'How to Control . . .' But I can't help enjoying them, because they are short-lived and they are much prettier than the other weeds that infest the Hill.

In the country, having weeds is a bit like your children having hair lice. Or turning up for a date night with herpes. It's not done. Your neighbours, and indeed government authorities, will think you are unkempt, if not unhygienic. You have not been diligent enough in your pasture hygiene and, what's worse, you are endangering your neighbours. Like scabies under a blanket, weeds will spread to neighbours and the neighbours of neighbours. No fence will stop them.

Admission: we have Scotch thistle, stinging nettle, mallow weed, serrated tussock and a vine with scores of spiky yellow balls that burst open and spread hundreds of seeds every time you try to remove them. Those balls are called paddy melons, which is unfair to the Irish, even if some of the early settlers did grow them in vegie patches. We've tried to remove the weeds, but it seems that, after two hundred years of these sorts of infestations, nobody has arrived at good solutions for weed removal.

Take, for instance, the thistle. It was brought into Australia in the early days, possibly as an ornamental plant or as a stowaway in bales of food shipped to our shores. It comes from Scotland, even though it is rare there and some say it isn't a native there either. It was declared a weed as early as 1856. So that's 170-odd years as a blight on the country.

Paterson's curse was brought in via mail order catalogue in the 1840s. Some believe it is named after the Paterson family of Cumberoona, who showcased it in their garden in the 1880s, but it appears it had been around the paddocks for half a century by then.

Stinging nettle is supposed to be a native but it has spread from its usual habitat of rainforests to, well, everywhere. Obviously, it stings. For a couple of minutes, in fact. Despite its vicious nature, you can buy stinging nettle seeds and grow it in your herb garden if you're the sort of person who likes eating kale.

Serrated tussock is a latecomer. From South America, it appeared in Australia in the early 1900s and may have arrived in saddle packing. It was first spotted in . . . Yass. Which is why it's sometimes called Yass River tussock. It's almost a native for us and, in fact, we've had more success in ridding the paddocks of it than with any other weed.

(Researching the origins of weeds is a fun exercise because there are so many versions of their history. It's as if everyone has tried to distance themselves from any involvement and pass off the blame to another farmer, a different decade or another country. But then, who'd want to go down in history with a curse against your name because of a pretty purple flower you planted in your garden?)

The serrated tussock was a victory for us, and it had to be because the local government department ordered us to get rid of it or they would send in expensive contractors to do the job and send us the bill. So we got a bloke on a quad bike to crisscross the Hill with a herbicide and touch all the tussocks with a wand. There's only a little of it left, on a hillock he must have missed.

The Scotch thistle we tackle by carrying a spade around the vineyard and beheading it before it gets to a flowering height. But you can't do that across 100 hectares unless you want to write Weed Exterminator on your tax return. So we slash as much as we can in late spring, but on the steep parts of the Hill, where no tractor or even motorcycle can safely traverse, we let it go. Please invent a better way to kill thistle.

The rest of the weeds—I'm sounding a little like I'm in court here—we tackle in more haphazard ways. We mow them, we spade them, we've tried sprinkling them with sugar, which is a method under investigation at the moment. With the stinging nettle, we've been told to turn it into tea. And drink it. That's what a bloke in the hardware shop told me to do when I asked him for a weed killer for stinging nettle. I guess he was being helpful, but I wouldn't drink that amount of tea in a lifetime. Unless I wrote Nettle Tea Drinker on my tax return.

The problem with all these weeds is that there is a solution, but the solution may be worse than the infestation. Roundup (basically glyphosate) kills just about everything and leaves the ground bare. But when you leave the ground bare, it's an invitation to weeds and, frankly, weeds are a lot faster at colonising soil than grass. Also, it's a horrible product. There are movements around the world trying to get rid of glyphosate. There are court cases in America awarding millions of dollars to gardeners who are dying from exposure to it; it is banned in some countries; there are scientists who blame it for the death of local ecologies. And, what's worse, my Mum hates it.

The case against glyphosate builds constantly. It is harmful to those who use it constantly and—legal note here—without protection. It not only destroys the weed, but it may inhibit the microbial environment of the soil. It's not good in waterways, but it shouldn't make it that far if you use it correctly. Obviously, it's not too kind on the insects in the area either. Some say it creates deficiencies that can only be fixed by further use of toxic chemicals. And, as I said, Mum hates it.

'It's against my religion,' she declared not long ago. She expanded, 'If I believe in the health of the environment and of my fellow human beings, then I can't in all good heart sanction the use of it.' Some of her farm helpers/managers (she has never given them a title) have used glyphosate to clear paddocks for the planting of feed crops. She wants them to sow the feed directly into the pasture, where it must compete with the existing grass. Less feed growth, but true to her religion. Sometimes she wins, sometimes she doesn't (especially when they think she's not looking).

Okay, we use glyphosate on the grow lines, but we have vowed to restrain the use of it. We use it around the youngest vines, so they don't have to compete with weeds or grasses in the first few years of life. And we only use it once a year. So, in two more years we won't be using it at all. The fact is that if you don't use it you have to do a lot more work. A lot more work. Using a whipper-snipper on a few hectares of vineyard is back-breaking. But we made a vow.

There's our dirty little secret. We have weeds, weeds that our neighbours don't have—yet. We are struggling to contain them, especially this year after the rains. And, when we do tackle them, we are using a horrible chemical.

But we're not alone. Australian farmers spend $400 million on glyphosate every year. It's applied across every agricultural sector and has been for sixty years. Even scientists who advocate a ban on it concede that it would have to be phased out because a sudden withdrawal would endanger world food supply. That's how much it's knitted into agriculture.

In the meantime, I carry a spade with me.

29

My BOM is Better than Yours

We were talking about the weather forecast with the viticulturalist when he said, 'There's going to be rain at the end of next week, so you'd better think about spraying.' Now we were ready to spray a sulphur and copper mixture to prevent mildew and had already done so a couple of times. But I was intrigued to hear his weather forecast.

When I checked my BOM app, the forecast showed only 50 or 60 per cent chance of rain and it didn't seem like much precipitation was expected. But at the end of the following week it poured.

The locals, I've decided, have a secret source of weather information that only they know. I recalled that at the end of the drought some locals accurately predicted a big end to it almost a month in advance. I had long suspected they had a secret source of weather information. Maybe a better app, or maybe it was the way they read the birdsong or the movements of worms in the soil. Maybe their dogs told them. Or quite possibly they had a telltale spring, like my mother's.

Whatever their secret source, there's something of a competition among the farming community for forecasting the weather. They talk about it a lot and, even if they don't admit it, I think they work out who's got the best weather-predicting skills. But then, this is not a pub trivia competition.

Farmers run their days, their weeks and the seasons on expectations of weather. That's sort of obvious, but it's not until you experience it that you appreciate how imbued it is in their timetables. Ergo, you won't get a plumber if rain is forecast for next week. You will be too late to source fertiliser, seeds or various sprays if your forecast of rain comes a few days later than everyone else's information. If you don't get sheep under cover in the day or two before rain, you're not going to get a shearing team on site. And, for wine-growers, you will not source the chemicals used to combat mildew or mould outbreaks if you are too late checking the forecast. There are scores more ways that a good forecast can make your farming life function better, but even in the most trivial of ways a forecast is important.

I was thinking about that this morning as I was training the new vines. Spring and early summer are their fastest growing period, and many seem to grow a foot a week. (To be precise, it's more like 8 centimetres a week). So you have to stay on top of their growth to get them in the right position on the wire. It's a bit like chasing an incontinent toddler with a potty. You'll get some, be too late for others and there will be a lot of tears in between.

We are behind with the training timetable because we couldn't get Brooke or Chrissie, who have helped us in previous years. As I was toiling in the field and muttering to myself about the lack of available labour, I was also eyeing off the dark clouds in the west. The air had a silkiness to it that seems to come with low temperatures and humidity. Maybe the feeling of silky air gives locals a heads-up on forecasts but then, if the dark clouds are already on the horizon, it's hardly a forecast.

The clouds had begun making noises. A low and distant grumbling. The light wind was on my face, so I knew it was coming from the west. Probably rain. But I wanted to finish the row. And another two, if possible.

I pushed on, wondering how far in advance of a storm lightning can strike. I knew it came during a storm and could come before a storm, but could it strike half an hour before the clouds arrived? Or even an hour? It was sort of important to know because vineyards are full of wires, and I'm guessing that lightning would find wire a pretty good target. Shiny metal stretched across a large field. Not much else to strike, except me.

I suppose a cautious person would retire at the sound of rumbling coming from dark—now very dark—clouds, but I'm not sure a lot of farmers would. The thing is that when you work on farms the work is outdoors (duh), and if you were to stop for bad weather or wait for good weather you wouldn't farm much.

We have worked in the vineyard in 40-degree heat, in 60-kilometre winds, in mornings so frosty you have to shove your hands under your arms every few minutes to maintain circulation and in soft rainfall that turns hills into slippery slopes. Even during insect swarms that force you to wear glasses, close your mouth and sniff out of your nose to clear your passageways. And sometimes we get to work when the sun is shining, the temperature is mild and the wind is a zephyr.

We work in weather in a way we never did in the city. We live in the weather in a way we never did. Weather is no longer just something that might force us onto the gym's running machine instead of taking a run in the park. It's no longer something that we check for the weekend's social plans. Or for a shower that might cut short a bout of weeding in the garden. The big worry about weather is no longer frizzy hair.

The rain gauge on our property is the first thing we check when we arrive, and sometimes when we wake. We work in weather and work with weather, and I guess that gives us a visceral feeling for nature and the landscape we work in. I think that's why lifelong farmers have weather-beaten faces: they have been sculpted by the sun and the rain, and by the squints at the horizon and the wind that brings the land into their eyes and noses and mouths and ears.

Judging by the state of my hands, I'm joining them in the cragginess stakes, but I doubt I'll ever be as prepared as they are. Because they hold the secrets of weather. They can judge the speed of weather changes and I'll bet they can tell a when a black cloud is the sort that could kill you.

The next time I checked the rumbling clouds on the horizon, they were directly above me and they had turned into a dark bruise. A crack of thunder announced the arrival of rain. I packed my secateurs into the tool pack and charged from the field, hoping I wouldn't fry because of my lack of weather-forecasting ability.

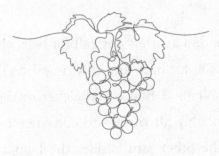

3 0

The Boys are Back in Town

Yesterday the plumber turned up. This alone was a cause for celebration. We wait for Jim a lot. So does my sister and, sometimes, my mother. I think half the town is waiting for Jim the plumber at any one time. Jim is always busy, but he makes an effort to get out to our place. He tells us this every time he arrives. Still, we wait. Weeks, sometimes months.

When Jim arrived, I threw my arms into the air in greeting. If I had owned a red carpet, I might have rolled it out. As I write this, it occurs to me that Jim might enjoy this prodigal son greeting so much that he keeps everyone waiting deliberately.

By the time Jim answers our call for help, there's always an additional job for him, and this time I had three extra plumbing problems. I had to be clever or diplomatic or pleading—probably all three—to convince him to do at least one of the other jobs besides the laundry waste job that he was here for.

When he was halfway through sorting the laundry problem (and well before he put away his tools) I approached him. 'I think we have a situation brewing on the other side of the house, Jim. Can you have a look at it?'

Situation was an understatement.

Jim followed me to the other side of the house, where a kitchen-waste-concrete-holding-bowl-thing-in-the-ground was oozing mucky fluids and smelling like a pig sty.

'I don't know what this concrete pit is,' I said. 'But it has a lid with a wire handle, so I'm guessing it might be something that needs cleaning. Every so often?'

Jim cocked his chin at me and lifted the concrete lid to reveal a soupy mess of washing-up water that contained bits of old meals that could well have been from the last four years.

'I can see what you've been cooking here,' Jim said, 'but too much of it is going down the plughole.'

I was just relieved that it was only kitchen sink waste and not septic waste that had backed up along the line.

That's if sewage can do that, which is another thing I have no idea about.

After a bit of tut-tutting, Jim retrieved a shovel and began digging out the mess and dumping it into a hole in the ground further afield.

I stood watching him and chatting. I'm not sure why I do that. I suspect most people would say thanks and retreat to a more pleasant-smelling corner of the garden, but I felt I had to bear witness to the mess our household had made. Or maybe, I felt I had to support him in his dirty work. In any case, I had to learn how to clean it in the future.

'You're not going to clean this,' Jim said, as he finished up. 'This is a job for the hubby.'

I was tempted to set him straight, to point out that women can do dirty work as well as men, that feminism has no demarcation lines. I was going to remind him that I was the garbo who had cleared hectares of junk from this land. But I hesitated. Sometimes it's great to be a woman, and I let him hold that fantasy for a while. Yet I knew that really I'm going to be the one revisiting this concrete pit.

❧

Jim's words flashed back to me last night when I met up with some colleagues from work for a dinner in the city.

It was a large gathering, so I was only hearing snippets of conversation. A group of the guys had been talking about their wives and how proficient their wives were at all those scouting-type things, like camping and knots and fires and hitching caravans to cars. And suddenly one of them piped up, 'What's the opposite of masculine? That's what I am.'

It was a strange thing to say, but I understood what he meant. He wanted to know how a man could describe himself if he didn't do traditional masculine stuff like knots, fires or hitching a caravan so it didn't come unstuck on the first corner. *It's not feminine*, I thought, as the conversation meandered around the subject. Feminine might be the linguistic opposite of masculine, but that wasn't what he meant. Besides, none of the guys in the conversation seemed particularly feminine. It's not wuss either, because only faux macho blokes with cheap haircuts and poor communication skills use that expression. New Age Man? Hate that expression; it reeks of incense and Bali pants. SNAG? Too 1980s, too fashioned by women. Metrosexual? Maybe.

The men around the table are all urbane, sophisticated. They have good jobs and successful careers. They are fit, into sports or activities, surrounded by active families. They like challenges, and their courage isn't lacking, because I know a few of them haven't faltered when called to fight injustice. Who cares if they don't know a double half-hitch knot from a slip knot?

As the conversation lapped around me, I reflected on what the men at the Hill had been doing that morning when I was leaving the farm: Jim digging out the slops from my kitchen waste pit, Roger jacking up the ride-on mower and fitting a repaired tyre to it, Ian carting old timber beams to make a bay for a concrete pour. If you work on a farm, there are so many ways to feel masculine. It's almost demanded of you. You might lift a lamb over a fence so it can join the flock. You hop into a five-tonne tractor to move earth around, or you spray vines or lift bales of feed for livestock, or shift stuff from one place to another. You use tools all the time. Big tools with giant buckets and heavy drills and levers that might be for lifting earth or might just change air-conditioning settings. You use muscles and knots and bits of wire that do the trick. You shoot animals that cause trouble. You grow meaty hands and wear a hat that bears the scars of all that work. It's the sort of labour that has defined masculinity and, in particular, Australian masculinity for centuries. It's a Frederick McCubbin image of the Australian man and it's etched into our national psyche. We all know a real man wears an Akubra.

In the city, there are few obvious ways of feeling masculine. The gym? Maybe, but women do that too. Sports?

That works, if you have the time and the mates to do it with. Cycling, running, kayaking, ocean swimming, boot camp—all those images of men in the city working hard at fitness are an expression of masculinity. Around my Sydney home, the roads are abuzz with men sweating bullets to achieve . . . something.

It's dangerous territory for a woman to talk about masculinity. That's partly why I didn't proffer an answer to the question at the gathering. But during that meal I got a glimpse of how tough it is for men in the city to connect with a sense of the masculine.

All the old ways of feeling masculine were born in the bush, mostly in the nineteenth century and, frankly, not many men in the city would miss those ways. Who wants to crack a snake's back with a spade or string up a freshly dead lamb for a barbecue? (For the record, no one I know has ever killed a snake. Relocated it, maybe, but not killed it. Possibly relocated it without its head, but accidents like that happen.) But city blokes know they're missing something. They sense that they need to find a lost identity. Or create a new one.

In the city, men can talk about identity, especially those men around that dinner table. They are erudite, aware of the waves of change that have washed over their workplace and homes and dinners. They are honest enough to raise it with each other and to leave themselves vulnerable to whatever answer is proffered.

In the country, I haven't heard too many men talk about masculinity. Maybe they lack the words; maybe they don't need the words. I have an image from a few months ago of ambling out to where Roger, Ian and Patrick were gathered around the utes near the shearing shed. I was attracted by their laughs and what appeared to be an interesting conversation. But as I approached, talk faltered, smiles were offered and two of them declared they should be off.

I don't have body odour and I'm not easily offended. I get it. They were talking men stuff. No, they were men talking about stuff. I don't belong there and I don't mind that because, geez, men need to talk and talk in their own way. If they're talking about machines or tools or the guy next door who stuffed up something, then they're being men. And they don't need words for that.

After Jim had cleared out the kitchen pit, I ambled over to where Roger was working on re-attaching a tyre to the mower. He was lying on a bit of old carpet, with a tool in his hand and trying to reach under the chassis. He looked like a mechanic. He looked like one of my earliest memories of his father—from the day we arrived at his home to find his father underneath his car, lying on a trolley with a wrench held aloft.

'Rog, you've done it!' I felt like yelling. 'You're the mechanic your father never knew!' But I didn't say this. Some things should be left unsaid.

I had hoped he was finished, because my pants were clean and I wasn't wearing work boots. He wasn't finished, so I knelt down in the dirt beside him and held the grease-covered wheel while he wielded the rachetting-wrench-socket-thingo. Then I walked back to the house with dusty pants, greased hands and another broken nail.

What's the opposite of feminine?

The Hill. This was the prettiest shot we could get of the farm in early 2017. The junk was big, small, toxic, ancient and so widespread it was visible on Google Earth.

From the top of the Hill, the setting sun casts the farm into shadow. The boulders look like they've been blasted from the earth. A rock farm, perhaps?

Home sweet home. The temptation to bulldoze the unloved shack was immense, and it would take years before we decided to give it another chance. Note the snake habitat.

Garbology: by this stage the blokes at the tip recognised me. I had become an expert on where to put timbers, wires, expired appliances, rank furnishings and green bottles.

The original shearing shed is a patchwork of corrugated iron, makeshift latches and boulder doorstops. But it has withstood a century of tough times.

A more modern shed (circa 1970s) didn't survive the tornado that swept up the valley. The tractor was extracted, and we made another trip to the tip.

The infrastructure for the sangiovese vineyard is almost complete. My daughter Kate, Roger and I can't wait for the planting of a thousand-plus vines.

My sister Mary and I plant the first of the sangiovese vines. It's hard to believe we did so much of it by hand, but the state of my hands affirms it.

The first clods are turned in the riesling vineyard. A horse would have been handy but Roger was up to the task. The empty dam portends dry times ahead.

A family effort for the planting of the riesling. Observe us discussing how to actually do it. Also note how dry the land is becoming.

Success. The crew gather for a hero shot after planting the sangiovese vineyard.
Not sure what the dog has in its mouth. Could be a rabbit.

A thousand white shields stand sentinel around the infant vines. Sort of looks like
a graveyard from this angle but most will survive.

The first frost. We never tired of going into the vineyard when frosts formed. Their patterns sometimes looked like star bursts or daggers, and once they looked like giant webs.

Shot on our way to a day's work. It was minus 4 degrees but we were determined to complete the winter pruning by September.

After just a few months, the vines peeked out of their shields. It was about this stage that we thought, *What do we do now?*

Ian, a man of many talents, explains the workings of his ingenious net spreader to me as the sun rises on picking day for the riesling.

My mother Ann shares a joke with her great-granddaughter Mila on picking day. At least Mila is impressed with the grapes.

Roger kicking back at the fire pit. We sometimes let the sheep into the vineyard during winter. We'd do it more often if the lambs didn't eat newly planted trees.

Homegrown roast. It's a joy to see hundreds of lambs skipping around the Hill. But I suspect this is the lamb who massacres my saplings.

The late summer sun rises on the vineyard, and travellers on the red-eye flight from Melbourne are streaking across the sky above us. I know where I prefer to start my day.

The room that looked like a prison canteen was getting a makeover. Such an ugly structure in such a pretty landscape.

There may be gold out there but there's not much wealth in a tiny vineyard. Note to self: that lean-to is leaning way too much.

Picking begins before the sun burns off the fog. Yohann, my son Toby and Roger are pumped.

Kate takes on the photographer with a mean pair of snips while her partner Yohann does the heavy lifting.

My son-in-law Paul tips the riesling grapes into a Nally bin. With such gentle handling, we might claim that our grapes are not just hand-picked but hand-curated.

Toby's girlfriend Georgie is dwarfed by a Nally bin of sangiovese and excited that the picking is almost done.

A heroes' roll call of harvesters. Yohann, Kate, me, Mary, my nephew Xavier, my friend Nick, my sister Wendy, Georgie, Toby and Roger. They get called heroes because no one got paid.

Bottled, boxed, stamped and strapped down. Now for the trip along a rutted country lane with the product of five years' labour.

Two years after the drought ended, the grass was English-standard lush, the sheep were fattened and even the ancient gums were regaining their glory.

A little too much rain in 2022. A record amount, in fact. The flood crossing at the base of the Hill was more flood than crossing for much of the winter.

At home in a wide brown land. *Credit: Nick De Lorenzo*

3 1

The Ghost Within

I'm edging into the haunted half of the house, room by room.

I start cleaning out the fireplace in the small bedroom, thinking I will simply dust it. But a duster doesn't do it. As I shovel through years of char and dust and suspicious-looking tails, I wonder what treasure I might find. A gold ring flung in anger? A fancy teaspoon? I find a fantastic blue-and-green bird feather and a bit of the bird that it came from. You never find anything of value in these humble old places, unless it's stuff that had no value in the old days but now has shabby chic appeal.

I empty the bags of ash and char onto the roses—pleased that I've created a micro carbon sink and soil sweetener in the one action. When I walk back into the house, I pause at the door of the decrepit bathroom. The builders are coming to strip it out in a few weeks and I can't wait. This little space, in the heart of the old house quarter, really looks like a serial killer shaved there. There are no blood splatters, but mould has formed like spatter marks on the ceiling, and with age they've grown scabrous. The fibro (asbestos) walls are damaged, and one section reveals burnt joists underneath. The toilet has a hanging cistern with a chain that lost its nob many years ago. The floor is partial. Part tile, part lino and, in parts, just partial. There is a small window looking out to the northern part of the 'garden'. It's a sweet window and I imagine Rapunzel storylines, even if it's not big enough for a slim princess to climb through.

The whole bathroom is going to be stripped out. Like a cancer that sits in the middle of the body, it is going to be excised—walls, ceiling, floors: everything except the little window will go—and I think the rest of the haunted part of the house will recover a little once this site of despair is gone.

So, in anticipation of the builder and plumber turning up this year, we have started renovating the substantial room that lies adjacent to it. I think this room, which has a jerry-built enclosed verandah at one end, was once the living room. That's partly because of its size but also because on the original footprint of this house there was only one bedroom, plus a living area, kitchen, bathroom and a funny-shaped open room that might have been an entrance or a baby's bedroom or small dining room. Re-imagining past lives through the footprint of this house is tough, but I'm not sure if it's a lack of imagination on my part or poor design on the owner's part.

The substantial room had a large plywood wardrobe that shook as you walked past. Roger and I demolished it with the blunt end of an axe and several pushes and shoves a few days ago. It had an old doona inside that stank of old man—everything in this part of the house stinks of old man. Once the wardrobe had been broken up, and I'd bandaged my little finger and cleaned up the blood, there was only carpet left.

Most of the carpet is a square of cabbage rose carpet, which was so popular in the 1940s. But obviously the owner couldn't afford a large square of cabbage rose carpet, so it is surrounded by a frame of crappy carpet squares around the edges. You forget how short of money and materials people were mid-last century. They were probably very proud that they got that much cabbage rose carpet for their house.

I want to keep that quaint centre carpet. But, when I remove the ugly outer frame, the rosy carpet looks frayed and adrift. It's also smelly and has puddles of old damp—I think the serial killer came in here after his showers. I tell Roger it must go too.

After it has been dragged out, the two of us crouch on the bare floor with pliers and hammers and begin pulling up about 835,092 nails and staples. It takes a whole day. By the end, my injured finger is looking infected and my hand will no longer fit into my glove. The floorboards, though, are virginal because they have never been polished. Even though I'd hoped for cedar or timber from a long-gone old forest, they are cypress—narrow-gauge boards that look sweet and interesting. Maybe shabby chic.

The walls and ceilings of both the bedroom and the verandah need to be de-moulded and bleached. It takes two anti-mould sprayings and, by the end, the glove material covering the fingers I use to squeeze the trigger has completely corroded. I suspect parts of my lungs have also corroded, but I'm not game to google the effects of 2 litres of anti-mould on lungs, especially as the fumes of two-and-a-half coats of white paint have yet to be endured.

Now the floor must be addressed. I'm tempted to leave it as unfinished floorboards. That could be industrial chic or simply lazy chic. But the boards look really thirsty. They make me feel thirsty, just looking at them, so they must be polished.

It would be nice to pick up the phone and ring a floor polisher, but I'm too embarrassed. I couldn't ask a tradie to walk through the derelict kitchen, through the sputum yellow hallway and do a good job on a floor that has clearly never been nourished. Besides, having worked this hard on this room—five days, one sliced finger and two corroded lungs—I want to finish it myself.

Roger and I hire a sander, get a quick lesson from the hire shop guy and carry 40 kilos of said machine into the bedroom. We stare at it for a while, wondering if it is going to eat the floorboards; however, it is surprisingly easy to operate and—after applying three coats of polish, a shade too glossy—the room is finished.

Well, almost. I paint the window frames and arrange for a glazier to replace the broken window in the verandah, where someone obviously tried to escape the serial killer.

By the end of the week, the bedroom is finished and the builder has stripped out the bathroom. I keep wandering into this part of the house to have a look. And it's not just to admire my work in the bedroom. I'm feeling much more comfortable being in a space where I used to hold my breath and squint my eyes so I wouldn't experience it too viscerally. I cursed this space. I swore demolition on it. I looked behind me for ghosts as I walked through. Now I can imagine a ghost gliding away down the hallway saying: 'What the hell have you done to my dosshouse?'

It no longer feels haunted. And it occurs to me again that haunted places aren't homes where the spirits of former residents wander—they are just places where there are no living spirits. The absence of habitation has a haunting quality, but a place feels normal as soon as someone begins to spend time in it, to work in it, to make it look more like a home and, even, to start to love it. Absence killed this home; my presence might restore it.

So, yeah, it doesn't feel haunted. It just feels like an opportunity to spend a hundred thousand dollars and lose the odd finger.

3 2

Plein Air

This is what exhaustion feels like. I'm lying on the couch, looking at the ceiling, arms flopped at my side and feet up on arm rests and still in boots. I don't move, think or talk and I would love to take my boots off because they feel as heavy as the concrete boots murderers use to sink bodies at sea. But that would require movement. Work boots are hard to remove even before they become dead weights. Elastic-sided, steel-capped and snug, work boots might be easy to pull on but, until they've weary with years, they fight removal. Pivot, suction, slow pull—they're tough bosses, resisting your attempts to take a break or call it a day.

I sip water. My constitution can't cope with anything more than sips. I should be hungry because I've only had a piece of toast seven hours ago, but I'm not. Even if I felt hungry, I couldn't get off the couch to tear off a piece of bread or grab a chunk of cheese, and if somebody handed me food I could only nibble at it. Constitution again. Not talking either. Too much breath is required for talking. I have no interest in anything except relief.

Feeling my body slowly stretch out on couch, throbbing feet akimbo on the arm rest, I have to remind myself that this is what exhaustion feels like, otherwise I might think that this is what dying feels like. I know—hope—that within an hour this will pass. But it doesn't feel that way. This must be what it feels like to be really old; this bone weariness, this depletion that can't be filled, this theft of breath and shrink-wrapped spirit. I might not be dying but I just got old really fast. Like this afternoon. Hey, it's 3 pm I'm now old. Pass me my cane.

We've been working with the vines. Pruning, training, thinning, stuffing shoots into high wires and managing the canopy. We shouldn't still be training and pruning: those jobs were meant to be completed in previous weeks, but they weren't. Well, we thought they were, but we are still too hesitant to impose the sort of disciplined cutting that is needed to produce the right number of shoots—roughly ten per vine with two bunches of grapes at the base of each shoot. We should have stuffed the canopy into the wires by now too—first the lower wire and then the high wire. We thought we'd done that too, but some of the shoots are metres long and they like their freedom. It didn't help that we took a ten-day holiday with the kids during the fastest-growing period in the vineyard. We arrived back to a vineyard that looked as if it had been partying through the festive season.

Apart from fixing previous mistakes and omissions, our main job today has been thinning the bunches and dappling the canopy. Alex the winemaker was firm when he visited yesterday to inspect the grapes that he will either turn into wine for our label or buy for his own label. 'Bunches should be thinned', he said.

Roger had been aghast. 'I'll have trouble doing that,' he admitted as he stared at the fecundity on the wires before him. There were bunches in abundance.

Some of the little ones, high on the shoots, had to go. We knew that. Some of the bunches lower down, which had uneven maturity, should go too. Fair enough. And the shorter and weaker shoots that had still managed to produce a few bunches also had to go, because a shoot needs twelve to eighteen leaves to feed a bunch of grapes and these little ones were trying to grow a couple of bunches with only a few leaves. We knew we'd have to thin the stragglers, but to grab a perfect bunch of grapes and chop it off seemed cruel.

The tough-love approach was partly due to the weather. A cool and wet summer had thinned the canopy of leaves and was slowing the ripening of the fruit, so we had to give the bunches extra help—even if that meant sacrificing the stragglers. I suggested Roger work elsewhere in the vineyard while the thinning was done.

My daughter Kate and sister Mary are helping with the thinning and both are artistic, so it's not surprising that we made it an art class. First the thinning of the leaves—a process that Kate called dappling. We tore off leaves around the bunches, careful to leave enough leaves to feed the grapes but strategic enough to remove those that block the morning sun. None of the leaves on the western side were touched because we need to protect grapes from the harsh hours of sunlight.

Once we'd got the dappling right, we appraised the bunches. And searched for the bunches. A lot were caught deep in the canopy, twisted around shoots and entangled with each other. These needed deft jiggling to free them from their mess; it was satisfying to finally see them fall free and hang low on the grow wire. Once we had freed bunches and removed the ambitious little shoots that had managed to produce a couple of doomed bunches, we decided which of the remaining twins to sacrifice. It was hard for all of us and sometimes—every few vines—we couldn't do it.

The result was satisfying. The rows started to look like postcard vines. The canopy was high and tight, and the grapes were draped along the grow wire, bathed in dappled morning sun and ready for picking. It almost looked like the grapes were on a shelf at the supermarket. This picking should be easy.

Kate and Mary occasionally stood back to look at their handiwork, leaning back in at times to pluck off a last leaf or jiggle a bunch. But my mind was calculating how many rows were yet to do, how long I was taking for each vine, how hot the sun was getting. I couldn't see the pretty result in front of me for the work ahead of me. I sped up. Tore, snipped, yanked, cursed. I was no longer an artist but a mad-woman on a mission.

Yet, even as my arms grew weak and my pruning hand swelled, I told myself this was not the attitude to take. I must let go of the idea that work can be completed here. It is never completed. You've just done everything you can do in the day. Or done everything you can do given your energy levels. And everything possible given your age. Oh, yes, that niggles.

As my anxiety rises, my footsteps slow. They trudge, more like it. That irks too. In the city you walk fast because you're trying to expend energy, burn calories and get that Fitbit wheel turning. In the country, you walk slowly, mostly 'cos you're fucking exhausted, but also because you know there might be another few hours of work that will crop up unexpectedly. Country conserves energy, city expends it.

All around the regions, work is slow this year because there are no backpackers or foreign students to help with harvests. The supply chain to pickers has broken, severed by the pandemic. Everyone in the regions is desperate for workers, but especially the farmers of fruits and vegetables— that sort of farming needs hands and strong backs rather than machines.

Country people who haven't worked in the fields for years, either because they are old or because they are bosses, are back on the soil. Some farm owners won't be able to harvest; others will only pick their most valuable crops. That means shortages of some fresh foods in shops and high prices for the produce that does make it into shops. At least Australians are realising how closely linked they are to the local food chain, how reliant they are on farmers, who normally barely rate a passing thought in the city.

As we close in on our first harvest day, we have been enticing family and friends to visit—and bring their secateurs and gloves. We are trading on goodwill and, even though I hate asking for help, it feels like a richer experience to have many contributors to the first vintage.

On the couch, after almost an hour, I have enough energy to check my Fitbit. Will it have completed its circles for the day? Will it declare You've Done It? Because nobody else is declaring that here. Will I get whistles and beeps and a hearty handshake from the energy keeper on my wrist?

Nothing. Not even a tiny movement on the exercise dial.

This device is telling me I have done no exercise, despite the fact that I've been in the field for almost eight hours, toiling, pruning, swearing, huffing, berating, wrestling, plodding and dappling. My right hand is now a size bigger than my left hand and there is nothing to prove it, track it, acknowledge it.

I am an ox.

And oxen keep working.

I feel recovered enough to slab butter and Vegemite onto bread and to feed it into my mouth. Food is only fuel. Water, though, maintains life and a functioning kidney, so I continue with the water. I will return to the field for another hour of work, but not until after 5 pm, when the heat begins to abate. I won't be dead, but meantime I will google to see if hard work kills people early.

A friend, a high-level executive, once said to me, 'Oh, you're a worker.' It was like he'd figured me out. More likely, he'd seen enough personality profiles in his HR department to recognise where I'd fit into a corporate structure.

I don't think he meant to be offensive, although some might take umbrage at his summation. I wasn't offended. I just thought, 'So, you noticed.'

I'm a worker. I'm an ox. And I'm not ashamed of it. Put me to work.

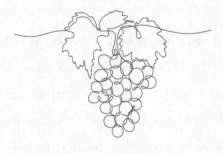

33

Netscape

The nets are on. In my mind that sounds like 'The Eagle Has Landed!' It deserves caps or, at least, an exclamation mark.

Of all the jobs in the vineyard, the laying of nets over the vines has loomed largest at the back of my mind. These nets are hundreds of metres long and about 12 to 15 metres wide, and they should be laid at a height of over 2 metres and stretch across two rows of vines, with walking room underneath. Then they must be secured with several hundred steel pegs on their edges because our nets are a bit narrow. It's like erecting the biggest tent in the world. No, it's like pulling a fishnet stocking over a landscape. And you'd better hope a ragged fingernail doesn't rip a hole in it.

For the past year, Roger and I have been talking through ways of getting the nets up. And indeed down, because we've been told there's only one job harder than putting up nets and that's pulling them down again. It has occurred to me that there should be a template for netting vineyards, given that there are 6251 grape growers in Australia and 7 million hectares of vineyards around the world, and nets have been used every year for the past century or so. Why do we have to reinvent the wheel?

It's partly because we are so small, and most of the machines that have been developed are for big vineyards and are too expensive for us. But it's also partly because the local vineyards seem to have developed their own solutions for the job. And each of those solutions is a little different.

Roger has been casting around for ideas and, inevitably, asked Ian to put his mind to the job. Being a natural-born engineer, Ian has been looking around at neighbouring vineyards to see how they cope. He's been mulling through the action that will be needed for spreading and the way it might be incorporated with a tractor, and—in true country style—he's been keeping an eye on stuff around his house and ours that might be used in constructing what's needed.

The method that Roger and Ian came up with is brilliantly simple and yet looks as if it came from a *Mad Max* film set.

The centrepiece—which might be patented one day—is the use of some old trampoline legs as the spreader's arms. These have been welded onto a tractor platform unit that Roger discovered at another of Mum's properties.

While we have the best device imaginable for spreading nets, we soon discover that the key to it all is in the unfolding action. I say *we*, but on the first day I had an engagement in Sydney and it was left to Roger, Ian and my sister Mary and her husband Stefan to pioneer the procedure. They had worked out that the nets needed to be folded into wool bags in a concertina fashion so they would flow out of the bags, through the large needle's eye at the top of the spreader and then be hand-pulled from both sides of the row so they cover the vines.

By the time I dragged myself away from important events in Sydney, it was an easy job. I got the task of ensuring that the net unfurled in a regular fashion. So I jumped onto the platform, checked that everyone was in place and yelled, 'Go!' Then I used my arms in a breaststroke fashion to smooth the distribution of the unfolding nets.

I can't take any credit for the success that day. But, after all the edges had been tucked in with pegs—again made by Ian—and the holes in the nets had been fixed with zip ties—an innovation of Roger's—the vineyard looked snug. Like a big baby wrapped up for sleep.

And now we wait out the final month while the grapes ripen under the shrouds that protect them from birds. We are just in time, because galahs and cockatoos are swooping above the nets, sensing the feast below.

꿏

We're not there yet, though. During this final month, there are still dangers. From birds, storms, too much water, too little water and probably something else we don't know about. We can only watch. And monitor conditions. Chase the odd bird out and hope that a snake doesn't get caught up in the nets. Hope that the enthusiastic pickers in our family will show up on the day.

And we can start imagining what this wine will taste like. What personality will our wine have?

Our wine might be pretty, or it could have attitude. It might be a sprightly number, or the loud girl at the party: all upfront, nothing underneath. It might just be lacking in character, which is most likely given the young age of the vines, but I hope it's not that flabby, distempered man who spits biscuits when he objects to something.

A wine, they say, is made in the vineyard and ours is almost done. We can only do so much. At some point the wine will become what it is going to become and we will just decide whether we like it or not, whether others will like it, whether it was worth all our love and attention—and whether it's worth bottling.

3 4

A Ragtag of Design

This is my architectural plan. There is an old bedsheet tacked up against the wall of the sunroom/corridor/ rumpus room (I still can't decide what this room is). The sheet hangs in front of the existing window; its sides have been taped to achieve the right width and its length has been hemmed with a few safety pins to achieve the right length. This is meant to give me an idea of the scale of the proposed windows, but it looks like a ghost trying to escape the room. I don't blame it.

Architecture has been my secret dream career ever since I didn't get high enough marks to study it at university (note for critics: when I applied to uni, architecture was ranked just below medicine and higher than law). Mum knows of my secret visions and over the decades has hinted that I pursue it in some form or other. I've never taken her hints—or my secret passion—seriously and that's mostly because I doubt my skills would ever match my aspirations. The bedsheet hanging on the wall, trying to mimic a window, would agree.

In my defence, I have tried to sketch a blueprint— representing the size of the room, the dimensions of its walls and the height of its ceiling, and calculating a rough ratio for the new windows—but . . . it's been a long time between equations. I have also solicited ideas from visiting friends and family; I have stood them in front of the windows and said, 'Just imagine this was your problem.'

I've gone online and searched under the keywords that might give a golden mean for windows in walls. I've searched online, using keywords such as 'how to scale a room', 'floor plans with dimensions', 'window placements in walls', 'ideas for enclosed verandahs' and 'architecture for dummies'. One of the articles was quite useful, and I bookmarked it. But it still didn't give the golden mean.

I have gone to our local library, searching for something called *Architecture 101*, which would skim me thorough the first year of a degree. There were so many stylish books on architecture that I got pleasantly distracted, but I didn't need a coffee-table book, I needed a crash course.

The only book that was useful was called *Shack*. It was full of houses built by hippies, and many of the shacks straddled boulders on the edge of cliffs or beaches. They were so basic I couldn't even spot toilet facilities. Still, there was something evocative about them, something calling me. They had integrity and honesty and a functionality that spoke for a simple life. They also had great views. My standards were obviously slipping.

What really haunted me about tackling this project was that I loathed the room precisely because the windows didn't suit the space. They were too high, too wide and reminded me of somewhere in a prison—a canteen or an exercise yard. Whoever had built this addition, forty-odd years ago, obviously got the windows from a demolition site and didn't care that they were like piggy eyes in the wall. I knew the windows were wrong, but I didn't feel confident that my choice would be much better. That's how I feel about architecture. I can identify when something is wrong—I'm a good critic of architecture—but usually I cannot tell you how to fix it.

So I rang a local architect. I felt like a failure, but I consoled myself, as I waited on the phone queue, by telling myself this was the sensible thing to do. No one should feel foolish consulting an expert. Besides, I didn't want to spend the rest of my life looking at these walls and thinking the windows are too high/low/wide/cross-eyed.

The sense of failure was short-lived because the architect said her practice wasn't taking any new commissions for at least six months and most firms in the area were in the same position. She suggested the name of a building designer and I rang her, but she also wasn't taking commissions. She wasn't even taking pleas. There's a building boom on and I'm late to the party. Back to the sheet on the wall.

When I heard a car pull up outside, I pulled the sheet off the wall before anyone could see it. A bed sheet is not a building plan. It's just a sign of desperation. But I have the gist, and I have a builder who has been willing to work off sketches drawn on the back of envelopes before.

This is already a wonky house. It's never going to make sense to an architect; it wouldn't even make sense in *Shack*. I'm going to have to work with the wonkiness and accept that the house will determine the blueprint for its future.

There is both relief and disappointment in this realisation of limitations. I'm relieved because I won't have to hold myself to an architectural standard; whatever the wall of windows looks like will have to be okay. But, along with relief, there is disappointment, and I think it has to do with control.

239

Architecture is all about control. It's about designing a way of living. The materiality of the practice guides the way people live in those spaces. The residents of a house might eat in the kitchen because the breakfast bench offers morning sun in mid-winter. They can be soothed by subtly lit rooms with cosy dimensions; they can be excited by the movement of light throughout the day or they can feel in control of their environment as they open windows, doors or louvres so as to manage the movement of air through their spaces. Architecture offers an opportunity to sculpt a good life. It is a gift of consideration for the residents. I've walked into rooms and thought, yes, yes, yes: this place has been imagined for a good life; this space knows what humans need; this space is human yet a little bit divine too.

Back to *Shack*. It looks fun. It's definitely on a human scale. Shacks are ingenious and honest and they also determine the way people live. A shack that straddles a boulder on the beach will prompt you to swim every morning; to wash off in a bucket; to sit on a rock at the entrance for breakfast; to whittle accoutrements; to cook simply, deal with waste wisely and lie in bed at night listening to storms, owls and critters as if they are at arm's length. And they often are.

Shacks have a space on the shelves of architecture. Maybe I should give them more respect.

Letting Go

Picking is only days away. It was meant to be days *ago*, but our winemaker said the grapes weren't quite right. Too little sugar, therefore ultimately there would be too little alcohol content. Ripening across the valley has slowed down too, probably because of the cool temperatures and wet weather of this summer. It makes for an anxious wait. In the meantime, anything can, and probably will, happen.

One thing for sure is that tomorrow is going to bring a big rain event—40 to 80 millimetres in twenty-four hours. It might not harm the grapes—they are tucked under nets—but it will plump them up with water. I can detect watery grapes in wine. I think it's in the finish: not as tight, not as lingering, the taste sort of disappears on the palate. But a big downpour could also bring an outbreak of mould on the grapes and no one wants mouldy grapes. Such unpredictability is in the nature of wine. Yet, even as I tell myself we should accept what the season throws our way, it's hard not to get anxious when the bunches are plump and perfect and waiting for a squeeze.

It's weird that I seem to be feeling flat just days before the finale of our first season. I should be flushed with excitement and nervous tension. Is this like the days before labour, when you can feel both excited but also so sick of it? Could this be pre-harvest ennui, or just a feeling of loss? We are about to hand over our produce, our hard work, our little red friends, to someone else. From this weekend, someone else will take charge of our product and our grapes will be in that steel tank we saw last year in the winery.

I'm nervous about what it will taste like. All along I've had a niggling thought at the back of my mind. What if our wine is crap? There's a lot of crap wine around. If you look at most wines sold for under $15—and I suspect that's most of the market—they would be ... Well, I won't call them crap, because most of them aren't flawed, but they just ... taste like crap.

My palate might be better than my winegrowing skills. Geez, what a terrible fate—to raise produce on your land that you don't like. It's like a parent who doesn't like the

242

looks of her child. Or like a writer who knows her reading will always be better than her writing. Or a design aesthete who has no idea about architecture.

Before I went into labour with my first child, I suddenly thought *What if this baby inherited all the ugly parts of me and her father?* I mean, neither of us is really ugly but we have ugly bits. Big nose, weakish chin, wonky eyes—I won't go into detail. Mentally, I got all our ugly bits and stuck them onto a face template and came up with a child only a mother could love. Maybe even a struggle for a mother. But Nicole was a lovely baby. Still is lovely. And, as soon as I saw her, I couldn't believe that I'd imagined that jigsaw of ugliness when I was gestating such a lovely looking girl.

The wine will be a jigsaw too, a jigsaw of its environment. It will reflect the weather: mild and wet. Very wet at the end. It will be a product of the soil: pH 6, never before planted or tilled, a loamy red soil with occasional clay and bits of granite that may have been blasted from the top of the Hill when it was a volcano (shortly before dinosaurs arrived). It will embody parts of the terrain: a gentle east-facing slope at the bottom of a conical hill, well drained, a bit bumpy in parts. It will show signs of its competition with grass and weeds; it will have something of its history of drought and minimal irrigation during the past four years. There are marks that we left too: the training style (eccentric), the thinning of the bunches (well done, according to our winemaker), the winter pruning. Our wine will be all that and more, once the winemaker adds his skills and attention.

We aren't losing our harvest; we're passing it on for finishing. We're letting it move on to the next stage. It's growing up now and, while we will have lost our little grapes, we will get to enjoy the wine it becomes. We'll invite friends over to share it. We'll offer it to buyers to sample. We'll keep some of it in a cupboard, like the first dollar of a new business. It's the end of its time on our Hill and the start of its life out there.

I mustn't feel sad. But I should feel anxious. We have just six to eight hours to pick about three tonnes of grapes. We have thirteen pickers lined up and no one, except Roger and I, has ever picked grapes before. But how hard can it be? No, my main worry should be keeping food and wine up to the pickers, making it a day to enjoy and making sure they'll come back next year.

The comment made by our viticulturalist Richard just a few weeks ago echoes: 'So,' he said, 'have you got your pickers lined up?'

The question wasn't polite talk. Because of Covid and lack of backpackers, wine growers in our region are stretched.

They are covetous of their pickers and don't share their list of pickers with anyone. Even their first names.

We are lucky. 'We have family and friends lined up for the day,' Roger replied to Richard.

'So, what are you going to do next year?' Richard retorted.

I think every small vineyard starts with family pickers. Then friends. Then they end up putting flyers on pub noticeboards around March each year. Or they keep lists of their own pickers to themselves. We've got to make it a great day.

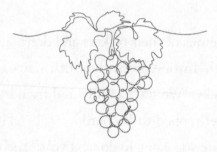

3 6

Harvest à Go-go

They're picked. Two-and-a-half tonnes of grapes from the vines of sangiovese and shiraz. Eleven workers, seven hours of work, music playing, cool autumn sun, soft grass underfoot, cakes for morning tea, a sausage sandwich lunch and beer afterwards. It could have been a French movie, except for the sausages (should have done a *ragout de lapin*—plenty of rabbits up the Hill).

It went so smoothly that it almost feels creepy. Like when you get out of the house with three kids so easily you think that someone must have forgotten their underpants. So many things could have gone wrong. And didn't. We were mostly worried about getting the nets off the vines, so we started the previous day, just to test our system.

The tractor with the Mad Max contraption worked perfectly. It was like threading a needle with a few kilometres of net. One driver, two net feeders walking along two rows of vines, and Ian pulling the nets back into the bale in a way that will make it easy for them to be spread next year.

Five minutes. That's all it took to get the nets off the first row. Five again for the second row. It worked so well we were confident of doing the rest at 6 am the next day. We held off completing the job because, of course, once the nets were down, the birds were free to feed.

The two nets across the top four rows came down at 2 pm, so Roger and I had to patrol the vines until sunset. We lounged around the fire pit with beers and a shotgun to scare the birds away. Picture-perfect hillbillies. Then we'd patrol in the buggy, or simply sit with a beer on the lawn and run like banshees every time the birds got close.

After four years we were so close to harvest that we weren't going to let the birds have a single grape. It reminded me a bit of the early stages of labour. Pacing the field, feeling an urgency, sensing a moment of arrival and yet being forced to wait. The sun set and we waited for children and friends to arrive for a late dinner and an early night.

The day began misty and calm, but by 8 am the sun was peeling back the fog and carloads of more friends and family began arriving. We had seven staying in our house (still no

247

second bathroom) and four were coming from their homes. We could have pushed for more pickers, but I'd figured there was a limit to the number I could feed, supply with equipment and manage. Management was going to be the key.

We had two suggestions for managing the picking. I'd thought we'd spread the pickers out over several rows and have a buggy driver weaving through the rows, swapping empty buckets for full buckets and taking the full buckets to the Nally bins on the back of the utes and emptying them. But Roger and Ian had brainstormed a system of having all the pickers working two rows of vines alongside each other and the tractor following with the Nally bin on its front prongs.

I got my way for the first few rows, because the tractor was still busy pulling nets off. And my system worked . . . okay. Then we tried the other way and it was so much better. Sure, it was more efficient—it involved less walking and I suspect it has been run that way in thousands of vineyards for centuries—but I think the main reason the shoulder-to-shoulder system worked better was because it was sociable. With people working alongside each other and on two sides of the same vine, you got to chat to everyone. It was like a speed-dating session. Or a stitch-n-bitch session.

Kate and I spent half a row debating whether the expression 'heard it on the grapevine' came from picking day in villages. Surely the day when the whole village turned up to pick grapes side by side would be the day you caught up on the gossip. A few rows later, someone said the expression actually came from the early days of the telephone in the US when the telephone wires were referred to as grapevines. I like our etymology better. The social system of picking might also have worked better because, working within a group, everyone sped up a little, especially as the tractor was always on the tail of the slowest picker.

We elected bucket boys to swap empty buckets for the full ones. I spent one row as a bucket boy and, while I was efficient, I sometimes forgot to be friendly. When Xavier, Toby or Nick took the bucket boy job, they made it fun. They'd crack jokes, gee everyone up and needle the tardy pickers. Harvest jesters.

At the back of my mind, I recalled the comment from our viticulturalist, Richard, when he heard that we were relying on family and friends for picking: 'So, what are you going to do next year?' Yes, picking is hard work, but it can be hard fun too. And when it's not paid, it can't be considered work anyway. It's helping out, and we humans do a great job of helping out.

Harvest. It has such a resonance to it. Everywhere around the world, it arrives with golden autumn days. It's the final day of hard work, the finale of a year's effort. And the first harvest is even more special. It's what you get when you've dreamed up an idea, found and prepared the land for your dream, planted the infant plants, watered and fed them, trained them, protected them from pests, diseases and birds, repaired them, supported them with wires or infrastructure and finally gathered enough family and friends to help you reap the bounty. I think we all felt the moment, felt embraced by the tradition—hey, we should have been in a French movie.

And it's just as well we enjoyed the process, because none of us was being paid and none of us was going to profit from it. I have to remind myself that no one really makes money out of vineyards, not the way we're doing it. Let me do some sums. Of the two-and-a-half tonnes picked, one tonne will be bottled as sangiovese under our own label, and the other one-and-a-half tonnes of shiraz will be sold to our winemaker so he can use it in his wines. He'll pay $2100 a tonne, so that's about $2500 for the grapes we're selling him.

Now those grapes we picked for him took eleven people about three-and-a-half hours to pick. So, assuming that pickers get paid $24 an hour, that means the real cost of bringing in those grapes was $924. And the labour cost is just the end bit of the equation. It doesn't include the use of the tractor, the use of two utes and a buggy, plus petrol. It doesn't amortise the cost the winter pruning, the cost of the time spent stuffing the vines into the foliage wires, the four years of training the vines, the cost of fertiliser and herbicides, the cost of planting, the cost of the land—even that little bit of land that the shiraz grapes are growing on.

I think my accountant would say we've got a whopping tax deduction at best. Except we have hardly any taxable income to deduct it from. No wonder this is a rich man's hobby. That was our mistake—we didn't get rich before we planted a vineyard.

It's possible to make more money from the bottled sangiovese. But still, after the cost of winemaking, bottling, labelling, storing, distribution, the retailers' margins and promotional work, you're still left with a . . . whopping tax deduction. It's lucky there's a lot of love in that vineyard, because there's not a lot of money in it.

We felt the love. In the vineyard, sitting around afterwards with a beer (and, yes, champagne); at the celebration dinner in town; around whisky later that night and dancing under the moon until midnight. Thanks guys, for your work, your good moods, your jokes and your forgiveness of the grumpy bucket boy.

Roger has pointed out that, because we picked during a full moon and danced around the land at midnight, our wine might qualify for biodynamic status. Nup, I said, we didn't have cow horns filled with cow shit buried at the end of the rows. Maybe next year.

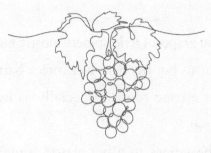

Illegal Still

The next day Toby starts making wine. This was not unexpected. We'd given him a 10-litre oak barrel for Christmas, thinking *Why not grab a few buckets of grapes, crush them with our feet and bung them into an oak barrel for a few months?* I was sure you could make something resembling wine that way, but I was also sure I wouldn't want to drink it.

Toby's approach to winemaking is like my approach to architecture. Go online, ask Google for a link, watch a few clips on YouTube and say a prayer. We are graduates of the short take, but Toby is feeling confident enough to begin.

Take two buckets of grapes and wash them. This probably isn't necessary, but Toby wants to drown all the spiders he's seen among the grapes. Little spiders mostly but, as he says, he doesn't want to put his bare feet into a barrel of spiders looking for an escape route. Especially as he is wearing shorts for the job.

We wash the grapes in a big plastic container and are almost finished when Roger walks past and mentions we are using the hose that is attached to the creek water supply and, given that the creeks were in flood last week and are generally full of animal waste and chemical run-off, this may not be making the grapes more sanitary.

We wash the grapes again, with water from the house tank. This has taken enough time for me to realise that there are a lot of little spiders hiding among the grapes and I wonder why we didn't encounter more of them while we were picking. I begin to feel itchy.

Having washed and drip-dried the grapes, they are now looking pretty in a 35-litre container. So Toby and his girlfriend Georgie scrub their feet and legs and take the plunge.

It is mesmerising watching grapes turn to juice. You can almost hear the pop as they burst and release a pinkish liquid. The juice is pink at first, but—as each minute passes and the bunches disappear beneath feet—the juice darkens, turning a frothy crimson colour.

It takes ten minutes of stomping, giggling, jigging and attempts at Italian songs for the bunches to totally disappear. Toby and Georgie hop out and then begin the more boring process of removing the stems. In wineries this is done by machine, but not here. The stems must be removed, but the skins should remain (YouTube again). When all the stems and spiders have been removed, they pour the juice into a large plastic container and discover they have exactly 10 litres of juice.

A few hours later, when Toby is riding home with friends, he rings a winemaker friend, Chris, and says words to the effect of: 'Hey Chris, I know you studied winemaking for four years, but can you tell me in twenty minutes or less how to make wine?'

I bet Chris loves calls like that, given that a few of his friends are thinking of getting into the Maker movement, where city professionals get in touch with their crafty genes on the weekend by making pottery, cheese, art, furniture, tyre art or whatever. I'm sounding cynical, but I totally get it.

Chris is generous and strips down four years of study and fifteen years of winemaking experience into something Toby can do in his flat back in Sydney. The winemaking community is generous with newcomers, even those who might just want a 10-litre barrel of homegrown shiraz to sit on their sideboard at the next party. Earlier that day,

Roger had visited Alex's winery to return Nally bins (and check how our grapes were doing in their new home) and asked one of the winemakers at the winery if she had any tips for Toby. She did and she also gave him a zip-lock bag of sulphites and a refrigerated container of yeast. So Toby is travelling home with a 10-litre container of juice, two bags of additives and a twenty-minute lecture on what to do next.

☙

I get the first call from Toby at about 7 pm: 'I'm supposed to put the yeast into water that's 38 degrees, and I haven't got a thermometer.' He knows that I bake cakes, but I've never made bread, so the handling of yeast has escaped me.

As we chat, he discovers (on Google no doubt) that if you combine two parts boiling water with one part cool water then the result is water at 38 degrees. Done.

When he adds the yeast, he waits for the reaction. 'It's not happening,' he tells me.

'I think it takes a while,' I say while scrolling through search results for yeast behaviour.

This might be the worst Christmas present we've ever given him. 'Remember everything about wine takes time,'

I add, still madly scrolling. I think about giving him a precis of the four years when Roger and I have had to wait for something to happen but I refrain.

Half an hour later, he rings: 'It's working! The yeast is coming alive.' He mixes a bit of the grape juice with the yeast mixture (as Chris has suggested) and then introduces the yeast to the barrel so the fermenting process can begin. Done.

Well, not really done. For the next week, Toby is expected to cover the ferment with a tea towel and stir the mixture twice a day, to break up the crust that forms. 'It's like having a pet,' he says. 'Should I call it Rusty or something?'

Toby and Rusty settle into their eastern suburbs flat for the duration. Toby belatedly realises he can't leave his mixture for more than twenty-four hours, so his Easter break will be curtailed. The wine is coming alive—it's not a pet, but it's no longer a plant. What is it?

It's alive, it's morphing into something else, it's becoming what the grapes and Toby's TLC will allow. Toby's Terror Shiraz, 2021. It could be his entrée into the winemaking industry or, at least, an interesting drop at his next party. I just hope I don't have to find uses for 10 litres of vinegar.

Postscript. By the sixth day of fermentation, Toby detects a slightly vinegar taste to the ferment. He suspects that he exposed the brew to the air too much when he removed the crust of skins. Perhaps. But neither of us wants to be the one to declare that the juice should be tossed out. We talk, we wait, we think up labels for vinegar. And then he rings Chris.

Chris tells him he could make port out of the brew. Evidently port can be made with a combination of young (slightly vinegary) wine and brandy. Toby goes out and buys four bottles of very fine brandy (roughly $400 worth) and asks if I want to help. I'm at Woolworths when he rings, so I get a bucket and strainer and dash over to his place to make some port.

I don't think Chris told him the ratios, so we figure it out with a taste test. Pour, mix, taste, repeat. We could get very drunk here. Eventually we work out that one part brandy to three parts wine seems to taste all right, and that is roughly what we have. So we mix it up in a bucket and siphon it into the oak barrel.

I don't know if Toby is planning to do regular taste tests of the brew. I wouldn't if I were him. I wouldn't want to know. It's better to leave it resting in its little oak barrel, full of promise, than to test the reality of a hastily thrown together home brew. Or he could invite his friends around to taste his first harvest, fill them with champagne—lots of champagne—and then open the barrel spigot when they're legless.

I suspect the brew will be fine because when I tasted the juice there was only the faintest tinge of vinegar and, frankly, it could have just been the taste of young wine. But it's a brew. It's a home brew. It's going to be fine. Just like our wine.

Fermenting

The first question people ask after they learn that the grapes have been harvested is: 'How is the wine going?' The only answer we have is: 'We don't know.' We don't even know if that's a question that can be answered. We feel a little silly.

Well, we say, we drove our grapes to the winemaker's place in late March; the staff poured them out of the Nally bin into a vat and we said goodbye. We will get paperwork at some stage—or not—and we know that the juice will be there for a couple of months, fermenting in vats and possibly finished in a French oak barrel but, apart from that, we're ignorant.

Roger calls the winemaker to find out what the alcohol content is, so the label can be prepared. But really he wants to know how the wine is looking, how it's fermenting, whether it's in second fermentation, whether anyone has had a peek at it and whether it will win gold at the next wine show. We'd settle for something that tastes nice. Alex can't tell him much.

What I really want to know is: at what stage can you determine that a wine is going to be awful or nice? Is it possible to go through four years of growth, a season of grape ripening, a harvest, half a year in vats guided by a fine winemaker, a bottling line, a delivery . . . and then discover it's undrinkable? Or do they taste-test along the way and, if it's crap, take it out the back of the winery and shoot it?

Our wine can't be bad. It. Can't. Be. Bad. After all, the grapes tasted great. They were handled lovingly. The soil is healthy. The season was kind-ish. We were guardians to the grapes. And they are in good hands now. But it happens.

One of the small wine growers Roger met this year admitted that when he harvested his grapes he discovered they made crap wine. No one would drink it; no one wanted to buy it. He is remediating his vineyard, improving soils, etc. But still, what an awful discovery. Embarrassing. And financially challenging. This vineyard is only several hundred metres away as the cockatoo flies.

The embarrassment is the worst. I imagine all our friends and acquaintances, who know we're growing wine and are rooting for us, suddenly being polite when they taste our wine. 'Umm, interesting.' 'Could do with a few more years.' 'I love a big, smelly red.' Or, 'I think it needs to be drunk with food.'

Oh, how they'd struggle to find something nice to say. They might even buy a few bottles and take them to the next party they didn't really want to attend, where they'd tell people it was made by friends and then watch those people be polite.

'It needs to be drunk with food' is what wine peeps say when I announce that I don't like a red wine. And I do that often and not too politely. But, in my mind, if a wine needs to be accompanied by food, then it is a handicapped wine. It can't stand on its own merits.

I don't want a wine that needs to lean on a good meal. I want a wine that is so good that you can sit with it as the sun sets, looking out over a Tuscan-esque hill and not desire anything else in the world. On reflection, I'm quite bolshie about wines, even though my pronouncements are not backed by expertise in the palate.

But most people are polite about wines. The same people who will traduce a restaurant, diss a meal, slam a tourist destination, get catty about car models and swear by lettuce mixes will be coy about criticising wine. Maybe they feel they don't know enough about wine to be a critic. They're afraid they'll describe it as plummy when it's full of grit, or smelling of leather when it's more cigar (I get those mixed up). They might recognise (more than I do) that everyone's tastes differ, that a friend who likes a red so big and gutsy that you feel your mouth has been through a boxing match won't appreciate the silkiness of a pinot noir.

But I suspect there is empathy at play here too. Unlike barley growers or lamb producers, wine producers are judged by everyone for what they produce. They are judged for the state of their vineyard, the style of their tasting sheds and the size of their pours at the tasting tables. They are judged by the taste of their wines, their methods of growing and making, their use of chemicals, the labels on their bottles and their choice of name. Everyone has a view on wine, even if they buy from the bottom shelf. But most go easy on the wine producer, especially if they're standing in front of them at a tasting table.

A wine grower is something of a romantic figure in agriculture. We think of them as lonely figures in a vineyard on foggy mornings, wielding secateurs, winding branches by hand, tasting grapes and imagining their future in a bottle. We want them to succeed and we feel sad when they don't, and not just because our drinking future depends on it. I know my friends would be sad if we fail, but not as sad as us.

We tell friends that we don't know what the wine is doing. And we learn to live with the unknowing. But sometimes we want to hop in the ute, drive over to the winery and just eyeball the vat that holds our four years of labour and our future as wine growers. Give it a pat and say hello or something.

In the meantime, I start buying bottles of sangiovese from other areas—Australia and Italy. I should reacquaint myself with the grape, prep my tastebuds and get to know the competition so I'll know a good one when I taste it. I want this grape variety to be familiar, to join my family of favourite wines. I don't want to be the first to say, 'This wine needs food.'

3 9

A Name to Forget

Gang gang. No, not the pop sensation in Korea. No, it has nothing to do with gang bangs. Or gang labour. Or the youths who wear identical black gear, carry knives and make everyone feel nervous. It's not a bikie gang either.

It's a bird. A cockatoo. It's the faunal emblem of the Canberra region. And, until a few days ago, it was the name of our wine. It was on the label artwork and ready to be sent off to the printers so it could be pasted onto the bottles in two weeks.

It's in the past tense because it's no longer the name of our wine. We have just learned that another beverage maker has the trademark on the name. They didn't have it last year, when we first researched the name and, indeed, registered the business name. But they have it now, as we discovered when we applied for the trademark. We have just been told we can't use it. So, days out from the artwork being dispatched to the printers, we're scrambling.

Roger and I sit on the couch and throw names at each other. Birdsville. Birdland. Galah Gully. Galah's Run. Cocky's Lot. There are lots of birds on this property—including an especially large flock of galahs—but we are exploring the nomenclature of the avian world because we don't want to change the image of the bird on the label. We've got the bird image, bought from the artist; we like birds and they like the Hill. And that's all we've got.

But this pastiche isn't working. What about we forget about birds. Ann's Harvest. Annie's Run. There's something familiar about those names. And a bit naff.

What about Cockatoo Hill? It's the name of the Hill, after all. It sounds a little cheap, but it's authentic. And the stylish artwork will lift it out of the Dan Murphy's bin.

'What about Bald Hill?' I'm half-joking. Who wants to be reminded of hair loss when they're spending money in a wine shop?

We ask our (recently appointed) lawyer to check the trademark status of Cockatoo Hill. And we wait. We are a bit stuffed at this point. There are thousands of different wine labels in Australia, and thousands more beverage names, and to those tens of thousands of names—for wines, beers, spirits and other beverages—we want to add one more. One that hasn't already been taken.

How many ways can you label a wine—a red wine? I wonder if anyone has called their wine 'Red Wine'. Nah, the trademark people wouldn't let you do that. 'My Red Wine'? 'Your Red Wine'? 'Your Resveratrol'? 'Just Another Bottle of Wine'? 'Not Another Bottle of Red'?

'This Is Good Stuff, Bloody Buy It'. That's what you want the label to say. It's just that there are so many ways of saying that.

Note to self: it's ironic that we're language people and we've stuffed up the only literary part of winemaking. But I'm sort of relieved that we can't use Gang Gang. I know it would have looked dynamic on the wine shop shelves. It's modern. A little funky. But it took so much explaining.

Everyone wanted to know what the name meant. And that's great, because it gives you a chance to tell the story of the wine, but the story wasn't that compelling. The property is named after a bird—a cockatoo—but it's not the same cockatoo that is the native bird of the region and we haven't seen it in our vineyard. It's probably visited at some time over the past millennia, but we haven't sighted it. End of story.

The Cockatoo Hill name is more literal, less compelling. But, geez, the Hill is right there. It protects the vineyard from the westerly sun. It creates a warm pocket on its eastern face. It has history. And its own story.

We can't use that name either. It's taken, in one form or another, says the lawyer.

Now we're really scrambling. We are only four days out from the scheduled printing of the labels and we are out of names. We know we can't afford to search for too many more names, because the search process takes a while. And lawyers are expensive.

'Red Wine Redux'. 'Drink Me'. 'A Red Wine from a Big Hill'. 'R'uvley Ruby Red'. 'Sheep's Run Sangio'. 'Last Gasp Guzzler'.

We start thinking of awful names or, at least, names that nobody else would want. We're sifting through the rubbish bin of lost names, overlooked names, words that mean little, objects that don't relate to beverages. Phrases that could mean anything but will still annoy buyers, who don't want to say a sentence when they're buying a bottle. I'm not a fan of phrases that masquerade as labels, but now I get why they do it.

Then we think of the address. Our road has a weird-sounding name and everyone we've encountered pronounces it differently. One delivery driver even chided us for not knowing how to pronounce it and we'd deliberately said it phonetically, to help him find it. It could be a French word, because we know that a French family lived here for a long time. But it sounds like it could be from the language of the original custodians of the land, too. And that's a cool combination. It's got seven letters and that's a design plus.

I try to imagine customers asking for the wine and getting it wrong in so many ways. I'm a little chary because I've spent my whole life telling people how to pronounce my name. Then I ask Kate about it, fearing her design brain will groan. Weep even. She thinks for a moment and then says, 'Maybe the pronunciation doesn't matter. Maybe it's okay that everyone says it in a different way. It's wine, after all. Everyone has their own view on wine; everyone describes it their own way. It's wine, it's difficult.'

Gounyan Wines. We quickly research the name. And it has history, beyond its geography as a road that passes by the vineyard. This name marked the start of white settlement in this area. Mary Davis (known then, and now, as Granny Davis) and her husband George established their farm Gounyan Estate in 1828, just four years after Hume made his trek down to Melbourne from the known settlement of Gunning.

Granny rocked. She had lots of children (six were marked in census records, but local history claims she had

ten children), she acted as midwife to labouring neighbours, she lived for 103 years and, closing the ring of
celebrity, she is buried just up the road from the vineyard.
Her farm was large and enlarged by the sort of casual annexation that was common at the time and, while earlier settlers
ran sheep on their properties, I can't help wondering if those
four grape vines down near the creek were Granny's doing.

We're intrigued, so we make a trip to the tiny cemetery
where she is buried. It's only 200 metres from the vineyard as
the cockatoo flies. If you stand at the edge of our garden, you
can see the chalky tombstones peeking above the wallaby
grasses. After four years looking out over the hills to the
south, we discover the history of this area and the resting
place of its matriarch.

If I feel slack about our haphazard approach to this
enterprise, I am reassured by what we see on Mary Davis's
headstone. On the original sandstone headstone, it says she
died at the age of 113. On a more modern plaque next to it,
it says she died at the age of 103. It's the gist, right?

The name is available. We can trademark it. We
will trademark it, whether we like it or not, whether we
pronounce it correctly or not. Gounyan Wines is born.
A difficult birth, for sure. A rushed birth. I hope it grows
into its name in time.

4 0

Wine Prose

I like it.

Okay, that's not enough. It is a sangiovese that well represents the conditions in the area during 2021 and the soil profile of the Hill and the care and attention that has gone into its growth, pruning, picking and winemaking.

It is a good drinking wine but, if I'm sounding a little hesitant, it's because it's quite acidic, owing to the wet and cool summer of its growing period and the fact that it's off young vines and possibly some other reason I'm unaware of. But it's good. It has a freshness, an honesty, not too much grit on the palate and a pleasing touch of sweetness right before the acid at the end.

I'm still sounding hesitant, but I suspect that I'm not a fan of sangiovese. My palate is spoiled by too much pinot, which is such an easy drinking wine. But this is good. The winemaker, Alex, and his assistant, Leo, are pleased. Roger is pleased with it. Many, many other people will be pleased with it. Cheap. Well, cheap by comparison with other wines of the area. Good value is a better description. Only $28 a bottle (still to be negotiated).

I look forward to tasting it by myself, because my first tasting was at the winery in front of Alex and Leo and Roger at 8 am on a cold morning, just minutes before the bottling plant began processing our wine. No pressure.

I had envisaged tasting the wine with Roger in some sort of ceremonial way. In my mind, we'd get our best wine glasses, place them on the table with the unopened bottle and a few chunks of tasty cheese and crack the bottle open. I'd pictured taking our first sniff and looking at each other as we decided whether it was fresh, bright, complex or mushy. I'd feared that first sip. I'd worried it would be followed by a pause as we tried to decide whether it was quaffable, even drinkable, pleasant, interesting, in character or whether we should go to separate rooms and cry.

Instead, the moment I first tasted our wine was in a cold shed office with three pairs of eyes watching and the bottling plant ready to rumble. What was I going to say? I couldn't use my usual descriptors—words like zingy, dirty, hospital, barnyard, old lady's dressing table and mushy—words you won't find in a wine dictionary. I'd kept it short—bright, good fruit, tangy at the end.

I'm looking forward to tasting it with food. Oh no, I just gave the wine a handicapped label. But it's true. A fresh, lively wine can be tamed with food. Thank God it's not a big, blousy wine. Or a ruby wine—I hate them. They give you a headache while the wine is still in your mouth. To me, they're like a punch in the face. Slightly acidic is better than any of the alternatives.

It was a relief to see it start its run on the bottling line. Roger was nervous. He kept prattling on about not much at all. When I'm nervous, I want silence and focus. Roger chats through his anxiety. Not a good match. He also gets too close to me. And others. It's almost as if he wants a hug.

I would have given him a hug—if I hadn't been so bloody nervous. Roger has done a fabulous job of conjuring those bottles of wine from the rocky slope of a sheep paddock. It would have been a disaster if the wine was anything less than what it is.

We were quietly and anxiously chuffed, and the guys on the bottling line picked this up. It is a mobile bottling plant, so it's enclosed in a giant truck. I was discreetly taking photos of the start of the bottling—our boxes being snapped into shape, the labels being loaded into the system, the pallet of bottles being lifted into the plant. Then they asked if I wanted to get into the truck and watch it happen.

This mobile bottling is such a simple and well-designed process. The bottles get lifted up to the front entrance of the container truck, and workers grab the bottles and set them onto the conveyor belt. First, they are washed and flushed with CO_2 blasts. Then they travel along to a rotating conveyor belt for the wine to be poured in from the vat outside. Then the full bottles move along to the screwcap machine, which spins like a mechanical ballerina to close the bottles. Then it's onto the labelling machine and out the other end to the boxes, which are filled by two people and placed on the final conveyor belt to be stacked on pallets and wrapped in cellophane like a gift.

Our lot only filled one and a bit pallets. Sixty-five boxes, minus one bottle. That's 779 bottles. Cheap, cheap, only $28 a bottle.

❦

The drive home from the bottling truck is tense. Four years of our labour and tens of thousands of dollars' worth of investment is on the back of our ute, navigating dirt roads that have been gouged by the recent rains. I am on edge;

Roger is chatty. It reminds me of the dash to hospital when my second and most impatient baby was on the way. The road is long and our cargo is precious.

I am so focused on getting our bundle of wine home to the Hill safely that I notice every bump and hole in the road and gauge each one's depth and angle. I feel every corner of the dirt road and wonder how the wines are coping. I check the straps every few seconds, feeling the strain in them.

It's like being in a slow-moving accident. Every fibre of my body is attuned to the dangers around. The hazards ahead. The slow motion of the world unfolding. I'm weird. It shouldn't be this stressful, but I've probably been holding this tension for a while.

The boxes are unpacked at the house and stored in a spare room with removalists' blankets tucked around them to protect them from temperature variations. Tonight will be the wine's first outing. First to Mum—look Mum, look what we've made, can it go on the fridge door? Then we'll take it to a barbecue at my sister's place. Thursday we will take it to the local wine bar and see if they're interested in serving it to their customers. Then to our kids : 'Share this with your friends, and tell them how you helped this wine get made.' Then I must take a bottle along to everyone who knows what we have nursed for the past few years. And ask their opinion. Or not. Hope they are generous. Not too honest in their opinions. It's time to declare: this is our hope realised, please be kind.

It's fine. And soon I'm going to think it's terrific, I just know it. I will help it along the way with my enthusiasm. I will enjoy its personality—the young bloke at the party, freshly shaved, flash shoes but a bit of a mouth on him. Most of all, I will respect it for what it is. This is the wine that grew on a hill that has only ever known sheep. It grew with the help of lots of caring hands, it survived storms and drought and many sloppy knots, and it ripened during a wet and cool summer. It is its environment. It is its soil. It is what it is meant to be. Enjoy.

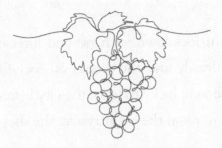

41

The Call of Country

A lamb is bleating at midnight. It is an exhausted bleating, like a newborn baby poised between crying and sleep. Except a baby's crying usually ends up in sleep.

It may be the same lamb that was going off last night. When I woke yesterday morning I had looked down to the lower paddock expecting to see a carcass and had been relieved to observe only a light frost and dewdrops hanging off old berries. I suspect the lamb has lost its mother.

There are many fences here and they are higgledy-piggledy, so the lamb is probably on one side of the fence and its mother on the other. The lamb is not going to work it out tonight. The vibe is forlorn.

Sydney is in lockdown with no end forecast. It's been three weeks already and the screws on social life are still tightening. We were lucky to leave the city before lockdown, so we are free to roam the countryside, the shops, cafes and even the pub.

Messages from Sydney friends and family are sad. It's wet, cold, boring and a little scary, they say. Stay out of the city, they say. I don't need convincing.

Being here in the country feels like an escape. Understatement. This big-sky countryside—with its air chilled off the mountains and its landscape devoid of people and dotted with fattening lambs—feels like the only place to be. Even if the lamb bleating down the Hill would disagree.

It's possible for the virus to spread in country areas—there have been cases—but the fact that it hasn't happened here during this outbreak isn't a surprise. There's space here, brisk winds sweep the main street, travel is in the cabin of your own ute and it's not unusual for country people to talk to each other at arm's length—a different take on a wide circle of friends. And then there's the propensity to spend time alone.

I wonder, as I hear ewes calling to their lambs in the distance, if there is an ideal amount of land that humans should occupy. There's an ideal space for cattle: one per hectare; and for sheep: ten per hectare. If you want a pony, you'll need half a hectare, although animals usually need at least one friend, so you'll have to double the area to accommodate two animals. There is an ideal number for wildebeest roaming the prairies and microbes feeding the gut; so maybe there is a certain amount of space that humans need to feel, well, fully human.

This desire for space has been shelved in modern times. It's not necessary in a world of global trade, industrial agriculture and computer programs that fulfil all your wants before you know you desire them. But I bet it's there in the less evolved parts of our brain: that sense that we need land around us to grow food; that idea that we like to see neighbours on the next hill, but no closer thanks; that comfort of having a small town nearby, with faces you recognise and a history that's shared.

※

I bought a stove today. Five years late. The old one was only slightly bigger than a camp stove and, if you turned it on, it smelt of meals cooked decades ago. I only turned it on once. After that, I used the microwave or barbecue. Or bought meals and cakes down from Sydney.

We have lived a camp-out lifestyle: microwaving cooked foods, barbecuing meats, going to the pub, fixing leftovers for lunch. It suited me, because I didn't have to invest in cooking accoutrements like pots and spices and recipe books. No expectations to be the cook here.

The stove was an impulse buy. I thought I was just walking past the local electrical shop, but then I walked in, found the smallest and cheapest stove and said, 'Can you install it tomorrow?' You can do that in a country appliance store. No global supply chains here. It's in the back of the shop and the guy who sold you the stove will install it tomorrow.

The first thing I'm going to cook is spaghetti bolognese, and then rock cakes to take to Mum. Rock cakes don't need a food processor. Or a fancy oven. They are comfort food from a long time ago, and I remember Mum spreading lashings of butter on them in the past. The only food she ever put lashings of butter on.

I'm toying with getting a washing machine. The plumbing for a machine is already in the bathroom and I'm running out of clean clothes. The idea of having a load of fresh washing flapping in the cool winds here fills me with . . . Joy? No. Satisfaction? Maybe a sense of home?

It's getting very domestic here. Very suddenly. It has been three weeks of camping out, wearing the same work clothes every day, doing a traveller's wash on socks and undies, keeping the going-out clothes clean. It's likely to be another couple of weeks. Maybe a month or two, before restrictions lift. Does a washing machine signal that this is where you call home?

My favourite washing powder is already in the bathroom cabinet. If a cop stopped me on the highway tomorrow and asked, 'Where are you from and where are you going?' I could say 'I've got a load on and I'm heading back to hang it out.' That sounds like home.

And when I cook the first batch of spaghetti bolognese on the new stove, I will have to buy thyme and oregano. I will then have a spice rack. If I decide to bake potatoes, I will have to use rosemary. Already there are cuttings of rosemary plucked from my sister's home growing near the roses. A herb garden, almost. Home is where the herbs are.

Herbs, washing powder, knowing the names of the trees in the paddock and the daily route of the sheep mob. It all sounds homey. It's what roots you to a place and makes that place seem like home. You grow into a home. You can buy a house or rent it and live in it, and it will feel like the place where you live, but a home is something that you grow into. Until then, it's a premises.

Yesterday a police van rumbled up the driveway and called Roger from the field. A neighbour—obviously not an observant one—had called police and said that Sydneysiders had just arrived. Not at all, Roger told them. We came three weeks ago for the bottling of the wine and we stayed for the winter pruning, and we don't intend to go back to Sydney during lockdown. He offered to show them a licence or the check-in history on his Service NSW app.

By the time I wandered onto the scene, the police were apologetic. They probably don't like dobbers either. I too offered my licence and check-in history, but I felt like saying to them: 'Look, I just put a new stove in; I'm researching washing machines; I have baking powder in my pantry and rosemary growing in the garden. I know where the sun rises at Christmas and what time the magpies start chortling at dawn. We have family here and we know the names of every crucial tradie. We know Ian.'

We are almost residents, even if we have no land title or work agreement. We may not be permanent residents, and we may never be permanent residents, because I miss my friends and family back in Sydney. I miss the ocean. I miss takeaway food and restaurants nearby. I miss the sense of having so much to choose from and the energy lift from being around the buzz of the city. None of that is happening back in Sydney now and the longer this goes on the harder it will be for the city to regain its mojo. So, officer, even if this might not be permanent, it is going to continue to be a big part of my life. My other home.

Oh geez, I hope I don't get seduced by this place. Because the work is hard and it's still not entirely me. My nails are ruined. I'm losing my posture. My muscles are getting toughened, but not in an attractive way. I don't wear make-up here; my one bra is only for going out; the only shoes I feel comfortable in are steel-capped. The rabbit-felt hat is no longer wobbly.

But I get why friends are jealous. I get why city folk are looking up real estate ads in country and coastal areas. This pandemic will change lives and, for some, it will change their mind about what they want in their lives. And what they don't want in their lives. There is a hankering for everything non-urban. For the space, for the different pace, for the sense of control over their patch, for the realignment of work in their lives, for the health of their children— away from hothousing to rough play, away from schedules to playing around in a paddock. Just away.

The lockdown has brought such tough controls on people's lives and freedom. Surveillance, movement checks, mandatory masks, rules (so many rules), restrictions, curfews, determinations of who is in your family, whom you can see, whom you can't see, when you can see them, how many of them you can see at any time and how close you can stand in relation to them. The view from the quarantine hotel is echoed in the view from the suburban lounge room; the view from the city to the country. In lockdown nation, everyone's view was looking out from inside.

I'm looking out of my lounge-room window at sheep making their way from the eastern paddocks to the west, bleating at their offspring as they mooch along. Little birds—finches and blue wrens—are darting through bushes, sensing that the days are getting longer and there is work to do. The flock of galahs swoops past, their wings sounding like the whoosh of a glider. A lamb is hanging around in the paddock out the kitchen window, not noticing that the others have moved on. It's probably that bloody midnight bleater.

The odd ute passes in the distance, returning from the day's work, crossing over the still-wet creek crossing. The land is plump with moisture, the grass still green. How green is my valley?

I get why others want to give it a go. I suspect that the biggest driving force—one that many might only intuit later—is the freedom that country offers. This is the last frontier, the place where you can gaze out on a stretch of land and imagine its future. Sheep? Olives? Barley? A vineyard? A bunker? This is a place where freed convicts reimagined their future almost two centuries ago. Maybe this will always be a place where you can imagine a different you.

It's possible. If a country-shy, sixty-something-year-old—with no idea what can be done with a piece of wire and no shame in admitting it—can do it, anyone can.

※

Three weeks on. Still here.

Four weeks on. The ceiling vent for the oven has been installed. Hassled the builder about installing a laundry.

Five weeks on. The woman in the cafe said, 'Hi, how are you doing today?' First time she's recognised me as a regular.

Six weeks on. I've started painting the outside of the windows. I never wanted to do this, but I figure it's better than whiling away time on a paint-by-numbers kit. Especially with my artistic skills.

Seven weeks on. A neighbour asks if I want to join the Facebook group of ladies who live along the road. 'We noticed you're living there now,' she says. 'Well,' I reply, 'not really living here. It's just for now and probably a bit longer. —but we're not sure how much longer.' I prattle some more. If I can't explain it to myself, how can I explain it to her?

Eight weeks on. It's been a whole winter here, the cops have lost interest in us and the weather hasn't been too bad. I wear a beanie everywhere. I have splurged on an oilskin vest and I haven't worn a bra for, ummm, I don't know how long.

Is this how it starts?

Epilogue

We met the neighbours a few months after the Facebook invitation. It was at a pub dinner to farewell neighbours who were moving to the coast, and every household along the road turned up. We bought bottles of sangiovese to distribute, but I felt guilty that this was our first attempt at neighbourliness.

Half a decade of observing their cars as they passed by the vineyard. We'd acknowledged them as they passed our place; the country salute—a raised finger—had developed into an open wave. But that was as deep as our neighbourly relationships had got.

In my defence, I could point out that we had been building a vineyard, ripping into a dilapidated dosshouse, coping with drought, getting to know tractors and weeding a few hundred acres. There was a cyclone, a few floods and a pandemic. We've sort of been busy.

Apart from discovering we have friendly neighbours, we learned more about the name of our road and, by the by, our wine. Evidently, *gounyan* is the Ngunnawal word for white baby (the spellings are as varied as people's pronunciation). That makes sense. Granny Davis was the first white woman to settle in this part of the valley and she did have lots of babies. Did they repeat the word so often that the Davises decided to call their farm Gounyan Estate? (Another local insists it's the name of the town that Mary Davis was deported from as a convict. I prefer the baby story. Like so much of the history around here, it's the gist that counts.)

The wine has improved. Like a distance runner getting into stride, the acid has retreated and other winey elements are coming through. It tastes more settled. Not sure if it's fit for a marathon, but it's got legs.

We've sold almost every box. Mostly to family and friends, and a lot was given away. We have three outlets in Yass, and a friend who runs a restaurant—and kindly stocked a few boxes—said one table of six recently ordered three bottles during an afternoon. Return customers are the best. We've had two good reviews: one in the local paper and another by a respected blogger. It might not be a fine wine, but it's a bloody fine effort.

Toby's port tasted decent too. Alcoholic, for sure, but he and his friends got through 10 litres of it in no time.

Ian is still with us. Not that he has been sick, but I have a constant fear that he might decide he's done enough work for us. Jim the plumber doesn't take so long to arrive, especially when he knows we've just finished another bottling. Daniel the builder is turning more of the asbestos dosshouse into a proud little cottage from plans that we both scratched out on the back of a cardboard box.

The sunroom is completed. The piggy-eyed windows have been replaced by bigger windows that some might say are a little Hello Kitty. And that's okay. The small room-entrance-way-whatever has been renovated and can now accommodate sleepovers. We have a deck on the western side, overlooking sunsets. The rank carpet has gone. The ghosts are gone too.

Snakes: we have seen none. Mice: more than a few. Birds: we are now able to name. Lambs: we are on our third lot. Weeds: still our shame—but the thistle didn't return as a carpet this year since the native grasses are giving it competition. Bathurst burr has begun appearing and, like every new weed, it's said to be worse than the rest.

Still no dog. Still feel guilty about that.

Mum visits, and mostly I have a cake for her to take away. She weighs too little and wears too few clothes in the winter. I want to plonk a beanie on her head, wrap her in a fleeced oilskin and lecture her on the perils of vanity, like her mother did when the teenaged Ann went off to a winter's school dance in a sleeveless dress. Pneumonia didn't stop her then; it won't now.

Friends have come to visit. A lot. They seem to like it here, even though we have to guide them up the rutted driveway, walk them through the derelict kitchen and try to ignore the snap of mouse traps that go off when we're halfway through dinner. We do simple things like talk, cook, drink local wine (very local), walk to the creek in the morning, play board games and throw skittles in the backyard. None of us has played table tennis yet, perhaps because there's too much eating and drinking, or perhaps our competitive spirit is dulled here.

During one such visit, on a kind summer day, I found the linen dress I had tucked away in the wardrobe years ago and was pleased to see it still fitted. I retrieved a straw hat that someone had left behind and donned a pair of sandals. Swish, swish. As we sat on the deck, sharing our wine offerings and gazing over the trees silhouetted on the distant hill, I thought *This finally feels Tuscan*. Then I thought, no, bugger it, this feels Australian. Noice Australian.

It's winter in the vineyard. Our fifth winter here. The vines need pruning. The rieslings are easy to cut, but the